I PEED & FORGOT

I PEED & FORGOT

An NFL father's apology letter to his daughter about facing demons and rising above failures.

Keyuo Craver Sr.

Copyright © 2017 by Keyuo Craver Sr.

Library of Congress Control Number:		2016917253
ISBN:	Hardcover	978-1-5245-5176-6
	Softcover	978-1-5245-5178-0
	eBook	978-1-5245-5177-3

All rights reserved. No part of this book may be reproduced or transmitted in any form or by any means, electronic or mechanical, including photocopying, recording, or by any information storage and retrieval system, without permission in writing from the copyright owner.

Any people depicted in stock imagery provided by Thinkstock are models, and such images are being used for illustrative purposes only.
Certain stock imagery © Thinkstock.

Print information available on the last page.

Rev. date: 07/11/2017

To order additional copies of this book, contact:
Xlibris
1-888-795-4274
www.Xlibris.com
Orders@Xlibris.com
733132

CONTENTS

My Greatest Influence ix
I Would Like To Thank xi
Prologue: My Daughter xiii
Chapter 1: Growing Up 1
Chapter 2: HHS Is The Best! 19
Chapter 3: There's No Place Like Nebraska 32
Chapter 4: To My Fellow Huskers And Aspiring Athletes 43
Chapter 5: From O St. To Bourbon St. 51
Chapter 6: Oh, Canada! 68
Chapter 7: Can't Stay Away (Back To Canada) 77
Chapter 8: I Never Saw That Coming 84
Chapter 9: Control 92
Chapter 10: What's Next? 101
Epilogue: Closing Letter 107

Dedicated to:

In memory of my father, Steve Craver Sr., rest in peace.

My Greatest Influence

So many people have played a major role in helping me learn how to set high goals for myself. Equally important, many have helped me learn how to push myself to accomplish those goals also. From the support of my parents, to the motivation I feel when I think about my kids, to my faith in Jesus Christ and the journey to seeking spiritual peace—there are so many great influences in my life.

Without a doubt my grandmother, Lear Savannah Craver, or "Madear" taught me how to be respectful of other people and myself as well. She taught me at a very early age that in order to truly appreciate something that you want in life, one would have to work extremely hard to value and appreciate it. Although she never attended a football game that I played in, she never missed a graduation of mine. She kept me humble when things were going great for me and always uplifted me when it felt as if the world was against me. She was my greatest influence because she lead by her actions. During my childhood Madear would always say a quote or an old saying which my younger brothers and I would not really listen to in depth because our minds were too busy being occupied by other things. Two of my favorites she used often when my brothers and I thought we knew something or didn't listen to her was, "The same thing that makes you laugh will make you cry!" and, "You may be old but I'm gray!" The older I get, the more I realize that she was preparing me for life lessons that would impact my family and me forever. To this day, when I make mistakes that I know she would not be proud of I hear her voice reminding me that she is still here watching over me.

KEYUO CRAVER SR.

I wasn't able to fully understand the magnitude of my grandmother's wisdom until after her passing in 2006. She was a great woman who was not perfect, but she treated everyone with respect. She worked hard to provide for her family and stressed the importance of God, family, and education. I hope and pray that I too have that type of impact on my family, as well as people I work with.

I Would Like To Thank . . .

First and foremost, I would like to thank my almighty Father in Heaven for allowing me to have the courage to turn this dream of writing about my life into a reality. I have strayed many times, but You have never left me and I honor Your leadership, mercy, love, and forgiveness.

To my three beautiful children, you all are my motivation to succeed—I hope you use this book to help you never give up in life. I love and cherish you with all my heart. You all are my greatest gifts, and I am extremely proud to be your father.

To my parents, thank you for always loving me unconditionally. Both of you have been there for me when I needed you most and have shown me the importance of keeping family close and loving one another no matter what we're going through.

Thank you to my grandmother, Eska "Momma" Moore, my mother's mom. Thank you for your strength, love, humor, and encouragement to stay faithful to the Lord.

To my three brothers who mean so much to me and have taught me so much, thank you. I thank you for our unbreakable bond. It's our time to teach the generations under us what we know.

To my nieces and nephews, it's your turn to carry the legacy and set an example for the younger ones under you. I love you and I am here for you.

KEYUO CRAVER SR.

To my close friends throughout my life, acquaintances, people who have sent positive vibes, I'd like to say thank you too. For better or worse, you all have played a role in me becoming the man I am and will become. While my mind might not have always been in the right place, my heart truly has been. My hope is this book will inspire people to always believe in their dreams and never give up on who they want to become in life.

RQQ to the Ques!

Prologue

My Daughter

April/May 2014

To my beautiful daughter, I love you so very much. I have never claimed to be the perfect dad. We have been through so much, and I want nothing more than for you to just hear my side of the story. First, I want to say that I feel terrible that you witnessed me so intoxicated. There are no excuses for my actions. Working long hours, going to school, and coaching a semi-pro football team eventually caught up with me. That night after you fell asleep I thought a couple of drinks with friends would be okay. I don't know why I think I'm Superman and always in control.

These factors, along with drinking took its toll on me. I remember thinking my day was starting just like any other morning. I normally wash my face, brush my teeth, and use the restroom every morning. In my mind, all of these things were happening until I realized you were calling my name. Suddenly there I was, using my living room table as a toilet. How embarrassing! Thank God, my back was to you and the table was all that I peed on, but you still didn't deserve to witness me at such a low point.

I'm not proud of the incident that morning, but I am relieved that it happened because I had no choice but to take a good, honest look in the mirror at myself, and my relationship with you. Knowing that I love you more than anything in this world, it hurts me deeply that you find it hard to believe sometimes. When you were born, it was sometimes stressful just to spend time with you.

KEYUO CRAVER SR.

This was mainly because two immature parents had to deal with the huge responsibility of having a child without really knowing each other. Early on, your mother and I spent a lot of wasted time and energy arguing. This kept our focus off of solving our problems, and created more issues for us.

I can't believe that I actually Peed in front of you. I Peed & Forgot because I was so intoxicated! What an idiot! How could I have let this happen? I could never live this one down, nor do I want to. Baby Girl, don't feel like you should quit on life when something goes wrong; try to learn from your mistakes and apply what you have learned for your next journey in life. God knows I'm trying to.

Despite my many setbacks and mistakes, God is the most important thing in my life. My actions don't always match how I feel, but I mean it with all my heart. I have faith He has already planned out your life and has put the right people around you that you need to aid you on your journey. He has a plan for you and you are His design. Never forget that you are a blessed child, and your light shines bright.

Often times our most negative situations ignite needed change in our lives. As kids when we wet the bed, it's so embarrassing to be called out by siblings or family members about the mishap. Although we feel like we are the only person to go through something so hard, truth is that everyone will have to learn how not to wet the bed eventually. For me, it felt like I was the only three or four year-old who had that problem, but I was not alone. There are a lot of people both young and old who still pee in the bed both literally and figuratively. Some of it is out of our control, but some is very much within our grasp. This awful incident that happened in front of you that night reminded me that I had forgotten who I was. Yes, I peed, but most importantly I forgot who I was.

I feel you have gotten different versions of who I am as a person, so I wanted to give you and your brothers something to have a better understanding of who I truly am, where I come from, and the people and events that impacted me along the way.

Love,

Dad

Chapter 1

GROWING UP

Growing up, it was tough knowing I was not as well off as some other families. Many would consider that I grew up poor. Although I stayed with both of my grandmothers growing up, confirmation that I was poor came when I was in third grade living at my grandmother's house in South Oak Cliff, Texas. My mom's mother, whom we referred to as "Momma," looked out for several members of our extended family. Momma's dining room area housed two entire families with multiple kids. Plus my aunt and uncle stayed in the same room too. Can you imagine ten to fifteen people cohabiting in one room with not much food, less money, and even less space? As a kid, we didn't quite realize the severity of our living arrangement. There were definitely some very trying times for us in that small living space. On the other hand, there were also some gut-wrenching and stomach-cramping times of laughter.

One particular instance I remember was when all the kids were in the bed. The adults were watching TV. My uncle Buck, who was lying on the couch with my aunt, attempted to quietly unwrap a candy bar. It got very quiet, because everyone wanted to know what was making that sound. My dad then called him out on it: "What you hiding over there?" he asked suspiciously. Once it was brought to light, my uncle had to share with everybody in the room—even the bad kids who only pretended to be asleep, myself included. These types of instances occurred all the time. Everyone was just trying to survive.

KEYUO CRAVER SR.

On the flip side, we found small things to enjoy. The roasting sessions were legendary and epic because everyone got involved. "Roasting" is when a person makes fun of someone to get a laugh at that person's expense. Many of the jokes were funny, but painfully honest. With ten to twenty people in the room at a time, we fed off all that energy and those times became cherished family events. Add in great cooking to go along with family who knew, loved, and accepted you for who you were made not having a lot of money manageable.

Saturday BBQ's were my favorite! Ribs, links, brisket, potato salad, baked beans, and deviled eggs with music, cards, and dancing were what made our family cookouts so memorable. Soul food is exactly what it sounds like. Being able to eat and share food, love, and happiness with family is what makes soul food. Our family has always been centered around our faith in God and love of family.

My grandmother, Eska "Momma" Moore, was a saving grace for us when I was younger. She welcomed my family into her home on several occasions and never asked for anything in return. She has always been a constant in my life, and I cherish her so much for the unconditional love she showed us. As I'm writing this, she is a spry ninety-something year-old with a great sense of humor that rubbed off on me.

Momma was also very smart. She sold all of us kids candy—we called her the neighborhood candy lady, but she had enough customers right in our own family that she didn't have to sell it to anyone else. With all that candy, her house was a kid's dream, but a parent's nightmare. She taught us to save our money so we could buy what we wanted. Many of us didn't have cash, so she started a genius IOU system. Anyone without money could get candy, but they had to write their names and how much they owed on a sheet on her wall.

One of my cousins somehow managed to rack up a bill for ten dollars, so she cut us all off until his bill was paid in full. Those were a tough couple of weeks, but we eventually were able to settle the debt by pitching in together and working it off doing chores around the house. Now that I look back on it, I can see that we kept my grandmother's pockets pretty healthy! Thank you, Momma, for your love, the roof over our heads, and your finance lessons.

I grew up with my parents, grandmothers, and a lot of aunts, uncles, and cousins. Although we were far from rich, my family had and showed a lot of love as I was growing up. We laughed so much as a family and even though 95 percent of the time it was at someone's expense, it was all in fun.

My parents were fun parents. Although they were pretty strict, they were both light-hearted and loved to laugh. This kept many hard times pretty light for my brothers and I. I think there were times of adjustment for us all when we were younger because there were a lot of kids and not a lot of money. My dad was an aggressive but extremely sensitive, charismatic Leo. He was definitely a kid at heart but was tough on us, too. My dad was the type of parent to get my brothers and me to go grab something for him from a room upstairs at our house, and once you were up there he would scream things like, "Freddy Krueger about to get you!" It was crazy. There you are a scared little kid, and you can't believe an adult would do you like that. Man, he was quite a character.

My beautiful mother is the quiet but strong force that holds our family together. She isn't one to use words to get her point across. My mother is a hard-working lady who never asks for help. Having a mother who loves you unconditionally is another of life's greatest gifts, and she was able to show my brothers and I that we all were very special to her.

I was the second oldest of four boys. We were all very different individuals. I don't understand how God skipped me, but all my brothers are six-feet-two inches or taller, and then here I come at five-feet-eleven inches. I guess you could say I have an issue with that, but overall, I was a very positive and happy kid growing up. I have always loved life and meeting people. On the other hand, even though I was too young to realize it at the time, I often pretended to be happy when I wasn't. Other kids got all kinds of toys, shoes, and got to go on trips, so I think a little jealousy made its way into my heart. Despite all these factors that felt like they were holding me back, I didn't take my frustration or anger out on the people I may have been jealous of.

KEYUO CRAVER SR.

I loved to laugh, and during my childhood that was such a blessing. I was able to turn a lot of negative situations into positive ones just by having a positive attitude. I attended Harrell Budd and Clinton P. Russell elementary schools in Dallas, Texas. I remember kids made fun of me—pointing at my shoes, making fun of my clothes, and even laughing at my haircut at times. It really hurt my feelings. I can see now that kind of suffering actually helped me. Because of those experiences, I grew in compassion and learned how to be less judgmental. I had to learn at a very early age that most people pick on and talk about others because of their own insecurities. Me being poor, and my dad being a horrible barber definitely made my younger brothers and me easy targets. But I would not change how I grew up for anything… it made me who I am.

My grandmother on my dad's side, who we called "Madear," lived less than two miles away, in the same neighborhood. The majority of our time was spent at her house, and our closest childhood friends lived in that area too. There were about seven or eight of us kids in the neighborhood who hung out with each other all day long. We did everything together! We played together, rode bikes together, and definitely fought together. Sometimes we fought each other, but somehow, we always managed to make up and remain friends.

There was one kid in our group who was a couple of years older than me. We were very competitive with each other, and for a few years we would fight each other for whatever reason kids fight for. And every year I lost! The last year I lived in Dallas before moving to East Texas, we got into a fight again. Despite losing so many fights to this kid, this time things felt different. Who knows why it started? I guess he felt he needed to establish his place over me once more before I left for good.

One of my favorite movies is "The Matrix" and its main character, "Neo," is who I felt like during this fight. I had lost so many times that I knew I wasn't going to lose again. When we fought this last time things were in slow motion for me. I saw everything coming and beat him to every punch. It felt like every kid in the neighborhood were there watching. I remember standing on top of this boy, just swinging away, but I really didn't feel any better. There was total silence once I snapped out of my rage and stopped punching the kid. I remember him rubbing his head and taking off running home. Seconds later all the kids started laughing uncontrollably, and I did too. Eventually the two of us made up.

I encourage you to avoid fighting a person physically at all costs because you never know the bigger repercussions that could come from it. I was lucky that it didn't go on any further than this. In life, no matter how old you are, you will have challenges that may be difficult to defeat the first time. It may not necessarily be in the form of a physical fight but when dealing with difficult people, like a teacher, a parent, or a difficult student who doesn't like you for whatever reason, you will have to keep fighting to get through it. Don't ever give up on yourself! No one is perfect. How different would the world be if some of our greatest inventors or leaders had given up the first time someone gave up on them? As long as you keep pressing forward you have a chance to change the outcome that you are faced with. Those troubles will become stepping stones to a better you if you face them and don't give up.

As a young child, I was able to recognize that I was a talented athlete. One early skill I learned that definitely was an indicator that I was gifted physically was teaching myself gymnastics at five years old. In our neighborhood, there were a couple of kids who were very talented at tumbling. Having that *exposure* to those talented kids at such an early age gave me the confidence to believe that I could become just as good as them.

Learning how to tumble gave me so much confidence. The more I practiced, the better I became. This also brought me more respect from the older kids who were better than me. In particular, I remember my older brother taking me to different neighborhoods once I had really become good and we would have tumbling "battles", pitting the best against the best, with about 30-40 kids watching.

Growing up in South Oak Cliff, I was bullied a lot. Tumbling gave me an escape, and I was able to make some good friends through it as well. Having this confidence gave me the ability to try harder in everything I did. I started trying hard to be a better kid in class, a better brother to my younger siblings, and a better person. When you do good things, good people will help you grow and *elevate* you as a person. I eventually was able to join my elementary gymnastics team as the youngest student in the group. Many people don't know that being a gymnast was my first introduction into organized team sports. It was an incredible experience and taught me so much at an early age. More than anything, besides learning the importance of being challenged and practicing to be the best, I learned the significance of being held accountable to your team.

Our gymnastics team would compete against very wealthy clubs from North Dallas, all with better facilities than at our school. On our team each member had a skill that they specialized in, and my two events were the floor exercise and the parallel bars. I actually loved competing and one thing I realized was that competition brought out the best in me. It drove me to really focus and try my best. Even knowing I had talent and trying my best, I also learned early that there would be times that I would lose. Losing did not feel good at all, but knowing that losing is sometimes a part of competition has helped me even more than just winning all the time. Many people don't understand that in order to be great at winning, you must be great at losing also. Losing helps build character and appreciation for winning. This also helps to have a better idea of how it feels when things don't always go as planned. In life things will sometimes not go as planned and being able to continue to work through that is a great indicator of a true leader.

When I was around nine years old, my dad ran into an old high school buddy of his that then coached for the Redbird Raiders, a youth football club in Dallas. Eventually my dad was talked into letting my brothers and I play. I was so happy and excited. It was such a surreal feeling to be playing a sport I loved so much with official uniforms and coaches. I was used to street ball or playground ball, with very little organization.

I was a gifted athlete, even as a child, so many kids accepted or respected me because of that, but I also drew jealousy for being the best at sports. I hardly noticed it, though, because I sincerely wanted everyone around me to be their best as well. My dad taught me how to be smart enough to humble myself, soak up as much knowledge as possible, learn how to play with others, and help make my teammates better. Although he was hard on us at times, I love and respect him so much for what he showed me in life.

I PEED & FORGOT

During my very first play in organized youth football, I caught a kickoff and ran it back one hundred yards for the touchdown. It was such a great moment for me. I knew without a doubt I was called to play football. It felt good to be validated. At that time in my life, at that age, everything was so new to me. I just loved to play.

Apparently, I was too young to know and understand the politics of organized sports, because a couple of months later my dad took my brothers and me off the team with no explanation. Not until I was much older did he explain to me that I was being treated unfairly. He said he didn't like it that the coach's son, who played the same position as me, always got to start. It wasn't until we were losing that I was put into the games. I wasn't even aware of this and didn't care. Later, my father told me he wished he had let us go through the experience anyway, to teach us about humility.

Right around the time my dad took us off the football team, my brother who was eight years older than me got shot twice in the stomach. That was the most terrifying moment of my young life—one of the scariest things I had experienced. I learned about what happened when my younger brothers and I were sleeping in my grandmother's living room on a pallet. My brothers were fast asleep, but I was only pretending. My father, mother, and grandmother were sitting at the dining table talking, and I listened to my dad describing how my brother had been singled out at a party and shot.

Not long after that, my favorite uncle on my mother's side was gunned down—shot in the head seven times. It was devastating for our family. Uncle Kip was loved by everyone in our family. Whenever he saw my brothers and me he would always give us great wisdom or put a few dollars in our pockets.

In light of these two traumatic experiences, my parents decided that we'd had enough, and we moved from South Oak Cliff in Dallas to a small town in East Texas called Harleton, a small farming town of about 800 people at the time.

About six months earlier, Madear (my grandmother on my dad's side), had moved back to her roots in Harleton also. With these deep family connections, this was a very pivotal move in our lives. All we had known up to then was South Oak Cliff. Needless to say, we were all skeptical of the move. My brothers and I had no clue what we were getting ourselves into.

It wasn't a surprise to us that we were moving to the country, because we had visited Harleton a couple of times before the move. However, we didn't really understand what that whole new world would mean to us until we actually arrived there to live for good. Despite our initial skepticism, my brothers and I were excited to explore this new beginning. We liked the idea of leaving the less-than-favorable conditions we had endured while on hard times in Dallas.

In Harleton, the houses were spread out, with so much land in between them. There is one traffic light and it's only a caution light on the highway that passes through town. It was fascinating for my brothers and me to have huge spaces to run around in and use at our disposal. And there were so many hay bales lined up in pastures! It was so much fun to run across them and pretend to play cops and robbers. Harleton drivers don't stop for pedestrians but they are more likely to stop for deer or wild turkeys. Squirrels are terrified of humans in East Texas, and are rarely ever in sight. As you made your way around, you could pick fresh fruit right off of trees and bushes just by taking a walk in the woods—pears, peaches, plums, berries, sourweeds, and you could drink water straight from a spring in our town. Lunch! We knew right away that life would be different there, and my brothers and I were completely fine with that. Moving gave us a way out of being bullied and being made fun of because we were poor.

It is also noteworthy to mention that by moving to Harleton, we grew up not far from one of the most famous places to get a hamburger in all of East Texas. Fugler's is a grocery store/laundromat. Bubba, the cook, is famous for his large, juicy hamburgers in those parts. If you ever have a chance to visit East Texas, stop by Fugler's, ask Bubba for a "Double-Bubba with cheese, bacon, and easy onions," and tell him Keyuo sent ya. I promise you will not be disappointed. (Sorry to get off track but I'm a foodie!)

Back to the story, even as a kid, I wanted to play professional football, so I took all forms of athletics very seriously. I saw it as a way out of "just surviving." As you can imagine, we stayed very active as kids in the wide open spaces around Harleton. I remember my dad signing us up for Little

I PEED & FORGOT

League Baseball not long after we moved. None of us had ever even held a bat or had ever worn baseball glove growing up in Dallas, but the game was huge in East Texas. My very first baseball game was so exciting for me. I hit two inside-the-park home runs! I remember hearing my coach say, "Dang, that boy ran like a scalded dog!" Our parents and our grandmother were very supportive of my brothers and me when it came to sports. Eventually my brothers and I moved in with our grandmother to help her around the house and for more stability for our family.

Imagine the smell of bacon, eggs, sausage, toast, and grits covered in butter every Saturday and Sunday morning as your alarm! The sound of bacon sizzling on the frying pan was one of my first true obsessions. Madear made sure every Saturday and Sunday that my brothers and I ate a good breakfast. She would just sit in her wooden rocking chair sipping a cup of Hills Brothers coffee and watch us eat with such joy and delight. It made her feel so good to see us enjoy eating up her food like that.

These weekend rituals were some of my fondest memories as a kid and looking back, I have definitely been able to understand the joy and greatness of being young and innocent. Having this understanding has convicted me to never stop a child from dreaming. My brothers and I had so many wild dreams as kids of how we would become rich and famous, and during those weekends, my Madear always had to listen to us try to one-up each other with our dreams. Although she may have laughed a couple of times during our conversations, she would always *encourage* us to do our best to achieve our dreams. It doesn't sound like much, but for a kid who truly wanted to be a difference-maker in life, it offered hope to continue dreaming. Her *encouragement* to dream big and to want the best for ourselves kept my brothers and me inspired and motivated children. She would always remind us that we could do anything and be whatever we wanted to be in life if we worked hard for it.

We also played video games, just as most kids our age did growing up. A few of our cousins would come over sometimes and play Sega or Super Nintendo with us from sunup to sundown. These video game battles would get really intense. There would eventually be a physical fight, or someone would get so upset after losing that they would cry and get made fun of until they left or until my grandmother made us turn it off. Those were by far some of the most innocent and fun times in our lives.

Growing up in a small East Texas town like Harleton was so much different from the city life in Dallas. My brothers and I made up for the lack of city action by using our imaginations. One of my brothers used to "drive" sticks and pretend they were cars. He took those sticks so seriously. He even concocted a knocker on the stick to represent the car's air freshener. When a family would come visit from out of town, their cars would be parked in front of my grandma's house, and my brother would park his stick with the other vehicles, as if it was a real car.

One time my dad ran over my brother's stick as he was parking his actual car. You should have seen my brother's reaction when he came outside and saw his stick, I mean his car, broken in half. He screamed and dropped to his knees as if it had been a real, horrific car crash. It was so funny to me, but my brother was crushed.

My other brother was even more creative. In the summer, both of us would "voice over" our cat, 187, and our dog, Bruno. I can't help but laugh when I think about the extremely high-pitched voice he used for 187's voice, or the screechy voice I used for Bruno's. We would dialogue for hours, speaking on our pets' behalf about whatever we thought was on their minds during those hot summer Harleton days. When you're not blessed with the year's top video games or toys, you have to be able to use a vivid imagination.

My brothers and I were considered good kids, for the most part. We made good grades and didn't get into a lot of fights. Living a good majority of our youth with my grandmother, Madear, we learned how to respect our elders. We answered our elders with yes/no, ma'am or yes/no, sir. Whether we wanted to or not, my parents and grandmother made us do it. That simple gesture in East Texas goes a very long way in terms of respect for the elders there.

At some point, I recognized by moving to Harleton we hadn't escaped being poor, but it was good to not have to worry about the unwanted attention or the persecution we experienced in Dallas. This is definitely why I empathize with less-fortunate people—I've been through it myself. If life doesn't present your childhood with a lot of money and material things, it can present a lot of unwanted and unnecessary challenges. This was the case in my family but luckily for us our parents taught us the importance of self-love and being able to get outside and explore things in nature. It was cost-effective for them I am sure, but it also taught us that we could still be happy and have fun without the newest toys or video games.

Harleton was totally different from South Oak Cliff neighborhood in Dallas. Harleton was a very small farming town, and the population of Harleton was literally black and white. I'm pretty sure there were mostly white people with a few black people in the town. I hadn't really interacted with any race other than the people in our predominantly black South Oak Cliff neighborhood, not until I moved to Harleton.

On the first day of school in Harleton, I noticed that the kids in my classroom were dressed like the kids in an episode of *Full House,* a popular show in the 90's. Everyone at the school was white, except maybe the five to ten black people I saw. I heard a student ask another classmate about me during recess, "Is he like Dante?" Dante was a former student who must have made a lasting impression on many of the students and faculty. The other student made the comment, "No, he is a *good* black student!" I'm sure he didn't think much of it, but I will never forget that day. I was confused by the statement, but didn't know or understand how to process what I was feeling at the time.

Little did I know this would not be the last time I'd hear the name Dante Jones. I learned from my classmates that before we got there Dante had been enrolled at Harleton Elementary in third or fourth grade, but transferred away not long after we had arrived. The students and some faculty at the school mentioned that he was always in trouble and difficult to work with.

I was happy to be seen as the "good" one, but I can't say that my childhood history is perfectly clean. For example, I remember the first and last time I got caught stealing. Madear took my brothers and me to Wright Brothers, the local family supermarket in our town run by good, hard-working people. She bought us each a Little Debbie® snack. I thought of myself as being slick, and I wanted more chocolates, so I stole a Snickers® bar. We left the store, and I got in the car, happy that I hadn't gotten caught. My brothers said they wanted to wait till after dinner to eat their Little Debbie snack, but I ate mine fast. My grandmother was a little puzzled. I told her I was hungry, and it was okay—I just wanted to enjoy it. I didn't think she knew anything about me stealing the candy bar.

I got home and was pretty happy with myself because I got my sugar fix and still had a candy bar for later. However, the phone rang while I was praising myself. It was the owner of the store calling my grandmother to tell her the bread man saw me steal a candy bar from the store. My grandmother was very disappointed and eventually, my dad had to be told. He was upset to say the least. Put it this way, it was the first of two lifelines that Madear threw my way in sheltering me from my dad's whoopin'. This event was very embarrassing for us in a town where there were mostly white people, and here I am representing my people, my family, and myself in a very negative light. I realized at that moment that was not how I wanted to be represented ever again. I'm glad it happened at a very early age, because it definitely showed me that was not how I wanted to live my life, and that stuck with me.

One would think racism would be very prevalent in a small East Texas town, but it wasn't. Don't get me wrong, there were some episodes of discrimination. One early memory involved a good friend of mine whose mother was a substitute teacher at our school. She was a beautiful lady and very sweet, and she loved me. I loved her, and I thought she was a great woman. In high school, her daughter, who was my good friend, ended up having a huge crush on me and we dated a little. When I learned her mom didn't really approve of it—only because of my race, it was very tough for me. I was hurt, and it made me feel ashamed that I cared a lot about this lady but she actually didn't really care about me. It taught me a very valuable lesson about race and acceptance.

In spite of all that, I can honestly say that 97 percent of the time my brothers and I didn't see racism directly. Most of the students were nice kids. When I did have questions about race or how I was being treated at times, my parents, mainly my father, would talk to me about those issues and how to navigate through them. He assured us everyone has a different journey, but he also encouraged us to not be afraid to speak our minds. He always made sure that we also showed respect to others whether we agreed with them or not.

My family was very supportive of each of my brothers and me. They were especially supportive of us in our academics. At Harleton, we received a great education. I was mostly an A and B student in school and throughout college. Harleton ranked very well in the state as far as testing went, and I am thankful for that. Having education support from my family and our school helped lay down a solid foundation for my future. As kids, we don't realize the importance of having basic education skills and how they greatly impact our way of living for the rest of our lives.

Over the years a few teachers really stand out because of the impact they had on me. For example, my second-grade teacher in Dallas, Mrs. Scruggs, was very strict, but she taught me how to take education seriously at an early age. My fifth-grade teacher, Mrs. Moore, taught me how to have fun while learning. She actually made learning easy and taught students how to be creative and enjoy school. Although there may have been teachers who didn't have my best interests at heart, most educational experiences I had were great, and I learned a lot from them. And then there are the teachers who have such a major impact on your life that it actually transforms you as a person.

Before they had what's referred to as the Big 3 in basketball, I had the Big 3 in academics: my English teacher, Mrs. White; my science teacher, Mrs. Greer; and my history teacher, Mrs. Pope. These three intelligent women taught me so much during some very critical years of my life. One of the Big 3 in particular, Mrs. White, had such a huge impact on me that even still, to this day, her philosophies and teachings play a major role in my life.

Mrs. White was my seventh-grade and eighth-grade English teacher. She was very passionate about education, and it showed every day. When I reflect on it now, there were so many things she did that set her apart. For example, one day during the week, we would always meditate to start the day. We were guaranteed one student, maybe more, would use that quiet time to pass gas for the class to hear. But seriously, at the time I didn't really understand the importance of training your mind and meditating to find inner peace, but on the days we meditated I always felt more refreshed and ready to take on the day's adventures.

Meditation is just one example of the many ways Mrs. White had an impact on all of her students. She was by far one of the most thorough and well-prepared teachers I have ever known. Like clockwork, every day was planned out, with activities and assignments back-to-back, from the beginning of the period until the three or four minutes left at the end of class when we would unwind and gather our things for the next class. She was so consistent. Not until I was much older was I able to see how having a plan and being well-prepared can help anyone become a successful person.

Without a doubt, the most significant lesson I was able to carry into my life from Mrs. White was her infamous "sir" and "ma'am" reference to students who used improper English when they talked. For example, I remember like it was yesterday being stopped in the hall by Mrs. White one day. She congratulated me on doing well on an exam I had taken earlier in the week. I made a reply along the lines of, "Thank you, Mrs. White. I ain't the smartest, but—" Before I could finish, she said, "Sir?!" Puzzled, I said, "Excuse me?" She then told me to use correct English.

With Mrs. White, you couldn't even go to the next question until you corrected yourself two or three times. In the hall that day, after two or three attempts on my part and Mrs. White repeatedly saying "Sir," I successfully repeated, "I *am not* the smartest, but I studied hard for the exam." Some of my classmates passed us as we stood there, and then continued down the hall laughing at me. Most of us tried to avoid Mrs. White for these reasons, but sometimes these exchanges were inevitable. She would literally pound you with "Sir" or "Ma'am" until you spoke the correct words. Talk about pressure! From that moment in my life even to this day, whenever I'm being lazy and using bad grammar, I still hear echoes of Mrs. White's high-pitched voice in my ear, saying, "Sir!"

Each of the teachers who influenced me taught with very different personalities and methods. One common theme, however, was that they all not only loved what they did they also loved the students, and we knew it.

I PEED & FORGOT

I want to take the time to thank the Big 3 for the foundation they provided in my development. I am so thankful I had the opportunity to learn from such dedicated educators, who set a great example for us during very critical years of our lives. Their classes were not easy at all, but their teaching philosophies were extraordinary. Thank you, thank you, thank you!

* * *

Throughout elementary school, my brothers and I were like most normal kids. We loved to play sports, enjoyed having friends over from school, and loved eating big bowls of cereal on Saturday mornings while we watched cartoons at my grandmother's house.

We often had visitors at home, most of them Madear's friends who would pop by frequently. Everyone who came to visit, no matter how old or young, was introduced by my grandmother and parents as "cousin so- and-so." I thought it was funny that all the black people in town seemed to be related. Not until many years later did I realize why this was the case. Many of us weren't cousins by blood. Sure, somewhere back in the lineage we might have been related to the people we referred to as cousins, but it was more just a way to identify with people who were close to our family.

Our life was very normal and common, but I did have a small brush with fame, which made an impression on me. When I was twelve years old, I got to meet Bill Clinton. Mr. Clinton was the governor of Arkansas at the time, and he was doing a lot of his presidential campaigning in Texas. When he came to Longview, Texas, our school went there for a rally with a lot of other schools. The rally was filled with hundreds of kids, and I was one of the fortunate ones to have Mr. Clinton walk by and give me a handshake. What a great feeling. It made me feel special.

With love from home and a solid school foundation, my brothers and I thrived in our new environment. Having Madear as such a constant presence taught me so much at a young age. She had lived a hard-working life, retiring after twenty years of working at TU Electric and moving back to her childhood home of Harleton, which as I mentioned is how our family ended up there. Madear was so serious at times but was just as silly and loved to laugh. She taught us how to take things seriously and also how to stay lighthearted during tough times.

Madear really loved to dance. When we were growing up, a famous rap group called Kid 'n Play had a dance out that became very popular. We watched the video with my grandmother and she told us, "They're not doing that right." Puzzled, my brothers and I explained to her this was a new dance. She laughed at us and told us the dance was as old as the hills. It was called the Charleston.

We laughed right back at her. How would she know? We thought she was pulling our leg. This woman then proceeded to bust out Kid 'n Play right before our eyes. We couldn't believe what we were seeing! Here was this seventy-five-year-old woman dancing the Kid 'n Play (or Charleston) better than anyone I've ever seen do it. She definitely earned our respect that day.

Just like my grandmother, I love to laugh, too. Anyone who knows me personally knows I'm as goofy as they come. The apple didn't fall too far from the tree. My grandmother really enjoyed my impersonations of the members at our church. I remember waking up on Sundays and listening to my grandmother critique what the women were wearing as they walked into church. We lived right across the street from our church, so we could see everything going on. Madear would say, "Sister so-and-so got that green hat with the beads, but her shoes don't match." She was such a fashionista, and was known for wearing her own fancy hats and shoes. Everyone that knew Madear knew she had style, and the confidence to go with it.

As kids, we met many great people who taught us and helped us grow as individuals. Not just teachers in school that I've mentioned, but also various teachers in life. At our church, we connected with a lady who I call Mama J. She was like a mother to me and we still have a very special bond that will always remain close. She used to tell my brothers and me that she loved helping us, because she could see that we were trying to make ourselves better; because we wanted to be better people. I respect that even more now because as a person who has worked in education, I know how discouraging it is working with students who have given up on themselves and don't really want help. It's very challenging to help someone who doesn't want to be helped. Mama J. played a major role in my development and in showing me that you can attain and enjoy the finer things in life if you want them.

Faith has also been a huge influence in my life. Growing up in the church was such a blessing, and it taught my younger brothers and I the importance of having a spiritual foundation. We grew up in a Southern Baptist church and were fortunate enough to learn the Word from a very knowledgeable pastor. The building was a beautiful small church with a huge white steeple on top of its roof. Also, the church sat on top of a hill, which gave it a majestic look that was peaceful and made me proud to be a member there.

I enjoyed church, but I was still a typical mischievous kid. For example, my friends and I sang in the choir and would always make my grandmother laugh by singing songs overly loud. We had no shame. We would belt out the notes, and I'd make sure to wink at her. She would laugh and nod from the pews, wearing a big smile because we actually didn't sound that bad. There were so many great moments growing up in the church on the hill and, without a doubt, I know I have been able to withstand some of my darkest moments because of what I learned at that church.

I was also good at imitating the elders, both men and women. When we went home after church, Madear would ask me to sing like Sister Johnson or talk like Deacon Cooper, and she'd just laugh so hard. I imitated men, women, and kids—from Deacon Cooper giving devotion to cousin Sally Mae catching the Holy Ghost. No one was safe.

Madear would even get me to do my impressions for her friends, too. It felt good to be able to put a smile on her face. One of her favorite things was watching me prank call her good friend, cousin Frankie Lee, using the voice of cousin Anna, one of my grandmother's other friends. Cousin Frankie Lee and I would carry on in conversation, and my grandmother would laugh silently while she listened to us. When I finally revealed to Frankie Lee that she had been talking to me, "Savannah's grandson," she would burst into laughter. When my grandmother would finally get on the phone, the two of them would just giggle and snort.

It's in large part due to Madear that my life in Harleton was so great. She was extremely loving and helpful early in my life. She taught us structure and how to do simple chores, such as washing dishes and clothes. We mowed the yard and raked leaves, as well. I hated doing those things at the time, but when I was much older and on my own I realized the importance of developing those good habits. God really used that dear woman to mold me.

Chapter 2

HHS Is The Best!

Fast forward to ninth grade at Harleton High School. A new student named Dante Jones arrived. Yes, THE Dante Jones, the one I'd heard so much about in elementary school. Let me just say, upon meeting this person the first week of school, I decided he was definitely one of a kind.

Although Dante and I were about the same size, he may have been a little taller than me. He was quite the character and without a doubt one of the funniest people I have ever met in my life. In fact, Dante reminds me a lot of my favorite comedian, Mike Epps, he was so goofy! I would say our interactions with each other started out okay, but anyone could see there was some competitiveness brewing between the two of us.

The stunts this kid pulled at school were like no other. With a serious face, he would do things like sit at the back of the classroom, ask a teacher for help with something, and then give himself a wedgie (or as we called it, a booty bite) as he made his way to the front of the classroom to the teacher's desk. All she could see was his serious face looking directly into her eyes, not so much as cracking a smile, but we could see the backside of him. The entire class would be trying not to burst into laughter, so we would be the ones to get into trouble. She would scold us, never knowing who the culprit was! This would frequently happen during serious class times, such as during the taking of a test. Dante just did things a normal person would never even think to do.

KEYUO CRAVER SR.

Our poor principal at the time was always put in precarious situations because of Dante. During football season, a bunch of us students were walking down the hall together as our principal was coming from the other way, toward us. Dante stopped, got into a three-point stance in the middle of the hall—like he was receiving a handoff—and then charged full speed at our principal finally juking him out at the last second as if he was playing against him in a game.

During basketball season, he would pretend he was dribbling a ball and then post up some poor innocent teacher and then either do a fade-away or back them down, turn around, and slam-dunk on them. These antics were some of the funniest things I'd ever seen anyone do. At first the teachers and administrators didn't know whether to laugh or suspend him. As time went on, though, Dante's tricks became so expected that it didn't bother school staff as much.

Anyone who knew me could tell you I was pretty easygoing in high school and got along with almost everyone. That said, there were definitely times early in our high school days that Dante Jones and I did not get along. He was the type of person who liked to push buttons. He loved finding out exactly what it would take to annoy a person beyond belief.

I don't know if he was jealous or had some other issue with me, but at first we did not see eye to eye. Yes, he was super funny, but at times he could be hurtful. Most students avoided or backed down from him, but I was never that type. We may have gotten close to throwing blows once, maybe twice at the most, but thankfully it never went that far.

Eventually, we got older and realized we actually had a lot more in common than not. He was an amazing athlete. He ran like a deer and was strong as a grown man. Honestly, he had more success than I did in football initially. In our junior and senior years, we both were the starting running backs of our team. I know for a fact that with he and I together, we were one of the deadliest backfields in all of East Texas. It was then I started getting a lot of recognition as a running back, and without a doubt, a lot of my success was due to Dante.

Not only was Dante a great runner, he was also one of the best blocking backs in the state. As I began getting a lot of recognition and attention from colleges, I never really got a chance to tell him how much I appreciated his selfless attitude but I truly am grateful for my time playing with him. I also have to admit that I am grateful for the adversity I encountered with him at first. Perseverance was definitely the key in our friendship, and I'm glad we persevered. To this day, he remains one of the most unique, and one of the top three funniest, people I have met in person.

When I look back at high school, I remember clearly the gorgeous summers in East Texas! Memories of summer days in Harleton were so beautiful and those times were so important to my development in becoming who I am today. From the smell of pine trees deep in the woods and along the narrow dirt roads, to the sound of 18-wheelers and big heavy-duty trucks flying down the highway—sounds and smells like these will take you back to certain periods in your life that you will never forget.

I admit, I was pretty mischievous on those hot summer days. I'm not going to say I was "bad," but I loved pushing it to the edge. I used to do crazy things in the country around Harleton.

Case in point, I remember one time in junior high, my friend and I had set a fire on a tin roof. When we were done, rather than leaving the remains of the burnt kindling on the roof, we kicked the pieces off the roof into a huge pasture that was right by my grandmother's house. It was a typically hot summer, so the grass was dry. Although we thought we had put the fire out, the wood was still smoldering, and within thirty seconds there was a huge fire. I jumped off the roof and tried to put it out, but my friend left. Once he saw the fire, instead of helping me, he just took off without me.

About two acres of land in all caught on fire. My grandmother saw it and called the fire department. Of course WE knew how the fire started, but luckily for us, there were a lot of fires getting started due to the extreme dry heat, so the fire department blamed it on that, and I wasn't about to disagree either. The whole incident traumatized me a bit at the time, but now that I look back on it I can laugh about my friend running away from the fire.

KEYUO CRAVER SR.

Years later, our high school basketball team was traveling to go play a district rival. As we were driving out of town, we passed Madear's house. As I looked out the bus window I saw my youngest brother and his friend at the same spot I had stood a few years earlier, also talking to the police and the fire department. They had burned the same exact pasture my friend and I had burned. My brother was way ahead of his time, as he talked to the police, he looked so calm. I just knew it was going to be a funny story when I got home. It was the same exact situation, same exact story, except his friend stayed with him, and they blamed the fire on someone throwing a cigarette out of a car that passed by.

One other particular Harleton summer really sticks out in my memory because I did something I never in my wildest dreams could have imagined: I actually broke a wild horse that grazed on our property. I didn't know anything about breaking horses, but we had wild horses that spent a lot of time on our property one summer. It started with my family just being able to see them, and then we eventually built up the courage to get close enough to them so we could talk to them without spooking them. Eventually, we were able to feed those horses as we talked to them.

One day, I decided I was going to try to ride one. My daddy thought I was crazy, but he was not opposed to it. I built up enough courage and strength to jump on this wild horse with no saddle and ride him just by his mane. I jumped on, and I was successful for the first couple of minutes. I don't know what spooked him, but he took off, not giving one crap about me on his back. He started bucking and sprinting through the woods. I held on for dear life, ducking under trees. I saw a big bush I thought would be soft enough to catch me, and I jumped into it. It was full of thorns, but I survived. So that's when I decided that driving a car was a much better mode of transportation.

I learned how to drive at the age of fifteen in a 1963 Ford Falcon, three in the tree. It was a three-speed stick shift, and was so cool to drive! After the Falcon I had a Buick Regal with a V8 engine. I also had a problem driving fast. In Harleton, there were no stoplights—just one caution light. One day, as I was leaving a basketball game in the Buick, I drove 120 miles per hour down the road, but I was caught by my dad.

I PEED & FORGOT

By the time high school rolled around, I was driving like a pro, but my tendency to push things to the edge and driving were not a good combination. In East Texas, the roads are very curvy and narrow. For a person who is just learning how to drive, they could be very intimidating, but not for me.

In my senior year, I went to a graduation party. It was my very first time drinking alcohol, and I stupidly got drunk. I was at the party with a girl I was seeing at the time. She lived in another town and, after we partied, I took her home in my grandmother's car and dropped her off. As I drove back to the party in Harleton, the alcohol fuzzed my mind, and I started going ridiculously fast on those narrow curvy roads.

I lost control of the car and crashed. So there I was, wrecked! By the grace of God, I had my seat belt on, so I did not kill myself. As it was my first time driving inebriated and I didn't know any better, I decided I was going to try to keep driving the car back to the party. Three out of the four tires were flat, so I was driving on rims, at nighttime, in the country, on the back roads, going about five to ten miles an hour. All I could hear was the loud, annoying scratching noise of iron on concrete, and I saw sparks coming up. After driving that way for about two miles I got back to the party at my friend's house. As soon as I pulled up they knew that something bad had happened.

"What the hell did you do?" someone asked. I just wanted to go to sleep, so I asked a buddy of mine to take me home. When we pulled up to the house, my brothers already knew something was not right. They were like, "You're an idiot." Even though they were too young to drive, they knew enough about cars to know I had done something stupid. And they were right.

Lucky for me, my grandmother was in the greatest of moods. She was usually in the best of spirits whenever she had visitors coming in from out of town, and luckily her sister and brother-in-law where visiting for a few days the next day. I was banking on that, so I waited till the next morning to tell her I had been in a wreck the night before. I told her I had to miss a deer, swerved, and went off in a ditch. She wasn't buying it, but she looked out for me anyway. Thank God she was my protector. She told me she wasn't going to let my dad come inside the house that day, because she knew he would probably have killed me. When my dad pulled up to the house, he saw that the car was not there, and he was livid. "Where the hell is Keyuo?"

My grandma, eighty-one years old, played bodyguard that day for me, a tough football player getting ready to go off to Nebraska on a scholarship. She said, "Keyuo is inside. He's good. You are not coming in. You are not welcome in this house." So my dad threatened me and left a message for me with my grandmother. "You let him know I'm going to get his ass, and we'll see if he lives."

The rest of that day, he did not come back to Madear's house. I learned later that he went to get my car, which was actually my grandmother's, to get it fixed. Later on that day, there was a phone call. My grandmother answered the phone, and I was looking at her because I just knew it was probably my dad, but she indicated to me that it was one of my coaches from Nebraska, just calling to check up on me. It sounded like a white man's voice, so I kind of believed her. I got the phone and said, "Hello." And low and behold, it was my dad disguising his voice as a white man's, pretending to be a Nebraska coach. As soon as I said hello, he ripped into me.

It was one of the hardest, if not the worst, verbal beatings I've ever taken in my life. He knew there was foul play involved in the accident and asked me if I wanted to ruin my life before it even started. He told me I was lucky my grandmother hadn't let him in the house, because he would have beat me black and blue. He just went off on me and rightfully so.

Those were some pretty crazy times I had growing up as a kid. As I look back on them now, and they definitely taught me some valuable lessons. I would also say they were indicators of some harsh realities I would have later in life as well. So make sure you pay attention.

When you're young, you don't really focus on what's happening now. You just kind of look for what's next. But I encourage you to take lessons from every situation you have in life and everybody you meet.

* * *

Although I had not really proven myself enough at that point in high school to foresee a bright future as a professional football player, it was always a goal in the back of my mind. As legend has it, football in Texas is like no other state. The relationships and rivalry between certain schools and towns goes back many generations. Although our team was not that great, our small town still supported us and came out to our games.

In my first couple years of high school, I was very mediocre. I didn't do much to separate myself from other athletes or students. I just depended on my God-given ability. I played football, basketball, and I also ran track, but I wasn't pushing myself to go to the next level in any of them, even though I had aspirations of one day being a professional athlete. Every summer, we would go to Dallas and spend time with my cousins and friends. It was a lot of fun, but there was really not a lot of structure. When in Dallas for the summer, I wasn't interested in keeping in shape for sports.

During my first two years of playing football, I did okay, but I had some decisions to make. How good did I want to be? That question really popped up the summer after my sophomore year.

My sophomore year, I was injured during football season. That year, Dante ended up taking my spot at running back, and he did very well. I mainly watched from the bench. It ignited a fire in me, challenged me, and helped me see that I wanted to be the best. Watching from the sideline definitely allowed me to realize that I didn't want to be a bench-warmer. So, instead of going to Dallas the summer before my junior year, I decided to stay in East Texas and work on my skills.

A big factor that also affected that decision was my sophomore year in track, in which I unexpectedly ended up winning state in the triple jump. I had the worst jump going into the state meet that year, but every week I was getting better. No one really believed I could actually win state besides my dad and myself. Everyone said, "Just enjoy it. Just be thankful you made it." But no one was really encouraging me to actually go win and bring a state trophy home. Amazingly, I was blessed and fortunate enough to win state in triple jump a total of three times.

KEYUO CRAVER SR.

It was through my faith in God and in myself, plus determination and hard work, that I was able to win that state championship, against all odds, with a jump of forty-eight feet as a fifteen-year-old sophomore. That victory was not only the most meaningful to me, but also was a turning point because it gave me the confidence to believe in myself despite the odds I was up against, and in spite of the doubters. Though I jumped even farther, over fifty feet, my senior year and set the state record for my classification, it still didn't compare to the feeling of winning state for the very first time. As long as I worked hard and believed in myself, I started to feel like I could accomplish anything I put my mind to.

Both my season on the bench in football, and my successful track season as a sophomore ignited a fire within me. Winning state was a very exhilarating feeling and all these factors gave me momentum going into my junior year. That summer, when I stayed home in Harleton and worked out, a group of us trained hard together every day, and it really showed as we got into our football season. I ended up rushing for 2,300 yards and 36 touchdowns my junior year, getting a lot of accolades and also a lot of recognition from different colleges. So, I set the bar even higher for my senior year.

Going into my senior year, I set some outrageous goals for myself. In an interview on the local news, I told the reporter I wanted to rush for three thousand yards and fifty touchdowns that season. He looked at me like I was crazy. I knew it was a very high goal, but "Why not set the bar high for yourself?" I thought. And I did reach that goal by the grace of God.

One of my favorite Bible verses is Philippians 4:13, *"I can do all things through Christ who strengthens me."* This verse reminds me that it was by the grace of God that I was able to achieve my outrageous goal of rushing more than 3,000 yards in one season, and making more than fifty touchdowns that same year. People looked at me like I was not human. It was a great feeling. Coming from my small town, a lot of people had never seen anything like that, so I was treated with a lot of admiration and respect.

* * *

During my last two summers of high school, aside from working out, I also worked for a man whose name was Mr. Wicks. He was a wealthy man, very smart, strict, but very fair. He used to tell me a lot of things, but one conversation in particular sticks out for me. He told me that in relationships, if I had a chance to marry someone, I had to make sure she was the same ethnic background as me. It used to bother me to hear him say that, because I was raised not to judge people by the color of their skin. It would take me years to understand what he meant and where he was coming from. I don't believe he was prejudiced. He just knew how society viewed races. He knew the reality that kids who were growing up with an interracial background faced and the struggles they dealt with. In Texas, to simply put it, there were just not a lot of open-minded people when it came to race relations. I definitely don't think people should limit themselves to a particular race when it comes to finding a teammate for life, but I have (as I have gotten older) gained a lot more respect for what Mr. Wicks was trying to teach me.

We did some good, hard work for Mr. Wicks. Seeing freshly-cut grass in large pastures, neatly bailed for moving, is one summer task I definitely will never forget. Bailing and hauling square bails is not a job for the weak, which I quickly learned the very first time my dad talked my two younger brothers and me into helping him. It was strenuous, hard work, and took all day. I coughed grass for an entire day afterwards, however the pay was pretty good to me. I learned to bust my hump in new ways that first summer working for Mr. Wicks, and probably not coincidentally, I had one of the best years as an athlete the following school year. I kept the momentum going and incorporated that hard work the summer before my senior year as well.

I know that learning to work hard contributed to a lot of my success as an athlete. Although it was difficult labor during those summers, it was a great way to bond with my family too. And the lessons I learned mentally and physically really showed up in my work ethic as a student and athlete. I am not telling everyone to go bail hay, however, sometimes doing things that are challenging, or not what we want to do, can also help you become better in the long run. I didn't want to do that grueling field work with my dad and brothers at first, but I kept an open mind and it has given me not only lifelong lessons, but also some of my best memories with my brothers and dad. To this day, I respect Mr. Wicks a lot and thank him for the work and for words of encouragement. Although I didn't agree with everything he said, he definitely played a big part in my life.

The towns we competed against were all small towns, with a lot of rich history and deep rivalries. It was nothing to play in a football game or basketball game and have someone call you the *N* word. I can remember a couple of different occasions playing against teams in towns like James Bowie, Texas, and being called the *N* word just because we were playing well. You might be walking to the locker room at halftime and a parent would shout out the *N* word just because you were giving their son a good beatin' on the football field or on the basketball court.

Dealing with that at a very early age definitely helped me learn to control my anger and be disciplined. I learned that some people will not accept you because of your skin color, even if they know you. So, I tried my best not to worry about it.

Going into my senior year of high school was like a fairytale. Everywhere I went, people knew me; people treated me like a celebrity. I was getting recruited by colleges from all over the country, and it was a great feeling. I came from a very humble background, so for the most part, I tried not to let that go to my head. I can remember a particular college in my senior year sending this beautiful girl down to Harleton, just to meet me and to talk about their school. At the time, I was young and wet behind the ears, as my dad used to say. I really didn't understand what was going on. My dad, however, enlightened me on the perks of being a great athlete and being touted as a recruit that many schools wanted. He shocked me when he said that if I wanted to "do anything" with that girl while she was visiting I could have had the chance. Luckily, I was scared and didn't know any better.

During the football season, it was like a fairytale, too. I cannot take all the credit; I played with a great, great group of guys, and I was just lucky enough to stay on track, stay focused, and make all the right decisions to be able to get out of the small-town life, because there were definitely guys that played before and after me who could have made an impact at a Division 1 school.

I remember going on my first recruiting trip during my senior year, which also was my very first time flying in an airplane. I remember just having a sense of freedom, getting lots of attention, and being away from home, and it felt real good. It felt like I was growing up, gaining independence, and becoming an adult. I was an offensive player in high school, but I knew going into college that I wanted to play defense.

I took five visits on my college recruiting trips, the maximum number of allowed official visits I could take, and each was unique and a lot of fun. I think that was when I realized that I liked to experiment with different things, open myself up to different experiences, and meet new people. My recruiting trip to Nebraska was unlike any other trip. I was able to come to Nebraska the year they won a national championship, which was such a great era for the program. I really got to see firsthand what the "Husker life" was all about. They made you feel like you belonged there and they also had very convincing staff who would not take no for an answer. During that trip, I got to see a significant amount of snow for the first time in my life.

Before Nebraska recruited me, I had gone on an unofficial recruiting visit to Baylor University to watch a game, and they happened to be playing against Nebraska, the eventual National Champions that year. On the field, I saw a Nebraska student-athlete working out and warming up, and for some reason I knew right then that was where I wanted to be. I knew I wanted to be a Cornhusker. Not even two weeks later, I got a call from Turner Gill, and I was finally being recruited by Nebraska.

Coach Gill was a Nebraska legend that was also from Texas. He had strong Christian values, which was what my parents and grandmother liked most. Coach Gill was also a devoted father. When I was young I didn't understand the time, and sacrifice it took to mentor and be there for so many young people, but I'm so thankful that I had the opportunity to watch, learn, and grow from such a great leader and a great man.

I didn't know until my playing career was over and I was being inducted into the Nebraska Hall of Fame, that the head track coach at Nebraska, Gary Pepin, had just as much to do with me going to Nebraska as anyone else. I was told University of Nebraska-Lincoln (UNL) was recruiting me for track, but Coach Pepin got in touch with the football coaches and asked if they were considering offering me a scholarship. Apparently, they didn't have a lot of information on me, but Coach Pep suggested they at least give me a look. I never formally got the chance to thank my track coach, but I am forever grateful for his influence and leadership.

So after they heard about me, Coach Gill gave us a call, watched some game film, and the next thing I knew, Coach Osborne and Coach Gill were visiting my small town. Are you kidding me? I knew I would be able to go play college football somewhere, but I never could've imagined getting a personal visit from two legends.

Meeting the two of them was a highlight for our small town and an honor. It was surreal. They toured our little school and met the coaches and faculty. They even talked to some of my teammates. After leaving the school, they followed my brothers and me to my grandmother's home. Coach Osborne and Madear hit it off right away. I admired how personal Coach Osborne was and, truth be told, my grandmother didn't really trust a lot of people. They talked about the old days, and Coach Osborne even bought some Watkins liniment from my grandmother. She sold Watkins products as a side job to keep herself busy. Coach realized she had been very instrumental in my upbringing and life. Coach Gill also made my family feel assured that I would be okay in Nebraska if I decided to come and play for the University of Nebraska-Lincoln.

They both made such a lasting impression that when other schools called or visited, Madear would throw it in the other coaches' faces that she had met "Coach Osborne and Coach Gill from the University of Nebraska" and tell them how great and personable they were. She liked the two of them so much that after their visit, she would even tell other schools who called for me that I was not home even if I was sitting next to her. She was something else.

After meeting with Coach Osborne and Coach Gill, I knew without a doubt I wanted to be a Cornhusker. It was a surprise to a lot of people, but I felt at peace with my decision. The recruiting process happens so fast, and if you're fortunate enough to have options, please consider them. Taking all five of my college trips helped me in knowing for sure that UNL was the right choice for me. Not only did I get to compete and play football at one of the best programs in the country, but I also got the opportunity to run track there as well.

Interesting fact, even though I attended school on a football scholarship, I won more championship rings in track than football. UNL also boasts one of the best track programs in the country as well as football. The shift in my life—going from small town Texas to a big-time university in Nebraska—all happened so fast, and I have absolutely no regrets that I chose to attend UNL. I also had no idea what highs and lows I was about to encounter.

Chapter 3

THERE'S NO PLACE LIKE NEBRASKA

Attending the University of Nebraska-Lincoln (UNL) was one of the best experiences I've ever had in my life. I had great teammates, coaches, great resources, and outstanding academic support. Even to this day, I am friends with many of the academic support staff, coaches, and counselors who helped me navigate my way through college. They actually cared about me as a person, as an individual, and not just as an athlete. I was also very lucky to have the same roommate in college all four years. We both came in the same year, were both from the South, and chasing our dream of becoming professional football players. Demo, which was his nickname, was very different from me personality wise but we got along well and had a mutual respect for each other. Those four years definitely would have been a lot harder for me if not for having a consistent friend and roommate. He is still my friend to this day and also the Godfather to my beautiful daughter.

UNL is not only a great athletic university, but also an outstanding academic school. My first semester, however, was probably the lowest achieving semester I ever had in a school year. I had a very low GPA: a 1.9 or 2.0, and it was not good. I was very embarrassed. I knew for a fact that my GPA was low, but I also knew I could fix it. After that very slow start my first semester, I refocused back into my books. I stopped partying, I stopped hanging out frequently, and I got back to being the good student I knew myself to be.

I was one of only three freshmen to play for Nebraska first year. We didn't have an exceptional season by Nebraska standards, but it was a great first year, and I experienced playing in my first bowl game. I was just thankful I got to travel the US, and to see what playing Division 1 football was all about.

I remember one of my first autograph-signing at Nebraska: people were walking up to me, asking me about Harleton, Texas, asking about my mom and dad, "Steve and Kathy Craver," and asking me whether my younger brothers were good athletes. That was so crazy to me; I didn't even know these people, but they knew all this information about me. It was a very humbling feeling. The people in Nebraska definitely take football seriously.

My responsibility to these dedicated fans was one of the reasons there was a lot of pressure during those years, but I've always accepted challenges and pressure. It definitely made me more accountable as an athlete and as a football player. Rather than going home during the summer, I stayed in Nebraska and worked out and got better with my teammates. I had a great summer working out before my sophomore year, and then I ended up having probably my best year as a Husker that following season.

Early on in my career I felt I had huge expectations to live up to. I was surrounded by great coaches and trainers, on an amazing team, with outstanding leadership. When I first started playing in this program, I was considered a weak link on our defense. This was mainly due to my lack of experience and also because I played alongside great players that were proven on the field. I was constantly being challenged and tested. Mentally this was very draining, but in time more strength and confidence followed. Being put to the test brought out the best in me, and there weren't too many things in this world that could compare to the thrilling pressure of getting ready for a game and the exhilaration of playing in front of 70,000 screaming fans. Truly one of the best experiences of my life.

In those early days at UNL, I had to really prove myself and gain the respect of my teammates and coaches. I felt so thankful to be at an institution where I was not only getting a great education, but was also becoming a better teammate and growing as a dynamic football player. As I mentioned, having supportive coaches and academic counselors who stressed the importance of being a good student as well as athlete played a major role in my development both on and off the field.

Playing defensive back isn't very complicated, but it takes a uniquely strong mental toughness to really be successful at the position. As a defensive back you have to be confident, calm, and able to shake off mistakes very quickly. This mindset also helped me in dealing with some of my toughest battles off the field too.

Summer conditioning and training is so vital to a team's success heading into the fall and bowl season. Many of my teammates stayed during the summer to get better, and we saw the fruits of our labors, being able to compete every year for a conference title. Being able to grow and learn with these young men taught us all so much about life and our own selves.

Since Lincoln was considered a small town, we had to find ways to keep ourselves occupied. We would usually play cards or dominoes at someone's house or apartment, and that would eventually turn into a pot luck dinner. With many of us not being native Nebraskans, we did things like this to have sense of connection and family. We did the best we could with what we had, and to this day many of them I am still able to call my friends. Although bodily appearance and hair color may have changed a bit, genuine friendships will always remain the same.

It's safe to say that it definitely took me some time to get adjusted to being on my own in college. Some adjustments didn't have anything to do with my time management, schedule, classes, or football. For example, one early adjustment that I still struggle with to this day is the boldness of the squirrels on campus at UNL. Coming from East Texas, as a country boy I was not use to seeing squirrels unafraid at the sight of humans. I remember eating lunch outside the Student Union one day and a squirrel came and sat right next to me, staring at me like I owed him something. It honestly freaked me out. I actually had serious conversations with my family back home about it, and looking back now I see that I really was a country boy.

Another confirmation of how much of a country boy I was happened when we played a game against the University of Texas-Austin my sophomore year. Prior to the game I had my mother cook me some chitterlings, which are pig intestines, and bring them to me after my game. I boarded our chartered flight so excited with my plate to enjoy on the way home. Almost everyone I passed on the plane asked, "What is that smell?" I had to explain what I was eating and why I would eat it to several people. I should also mention that at the time, I was going through a phase where I would wear this Raccoon hat everywhere. Imagine a nineteen year-old East-Texas boy wearing a raccoon tail hat, eating a plate full of chitterlings, sitting next to you on a flight home? One of the coaches laughed and said, "Keyuo, you really are a black cowboy!" Yeah, there was no denying it then. I just smiled and continued eating.

Almost my entire experience of going to college was great. Besides accomplishing a lot as a student and athlete, I also met one of my closest friends to this day. He was a African-American student who attended the university on an academic scholarship. Even before we knew each other personally, we would speak to each other in passing on campus, which was a little unusual.

You see, on campus, we athletes had most of our resources provided for us at our own separate athletic facilities--from lunchroom to study areas to computer labs, and dining areas where we would socialize. As student-athletes we were very well taken care of, therefore many of us never ventured outside of that area. The drawback to this for me was that I never really got involved or gave myself the chance to learn about different clubs and organizations available for students on campus. This alienation also very well may have contributed to miscommunications between minority student-athletes and minority students because we never really got the chance to get to know each other more personally. Many students that were not athletes felt as though we were "entitled" or thought we were better than the rest of the student population. There were instances where students would ignore me or just not acknowledge me when I would say hello, and after getting treatment like this a few times it had a negative effect on me too.

Not all students kept to themselves or made you feel alienated, and my close friend, CB, was one of them. I'm certain that we passed each other on campus sidewalks for almost an entire year, always with a cordial hello but nothing more, before we had our first personal conversation with each other. I was surprised to see him at an informational meeting for a Greek organization that I was interested in joining. We laughed right as soon as we saw each other and formally introduced ourselves. We both knew that we were there for a reason, and the fact that this man had enough decency to be polite and kind to a stranger that he didn't know made me feel comfortable with him. Our interactions on campus were very positive and set up a great foundation for a strong friendship. This foundation eventually helped paved the way for our journey into pledging and becoming members of the greatest fraternity in the world, Omega Psi Phi Fraternity Incorporated. RQQ!!

To this day he is one of my closest friends. He has seen me set and reach the pinnacle of my goals, and he has also has seen me fall in the deep pits of darkness. Like a true friend, he remained constant and never left or changed. The letters of our fraternity mean, "Friendship is essential to the soul." Through the tough seasons I've had, his self-sacrifice and self-abnegation demonstrated what it takes to be a true friend. We have been through a lot and he fully knows that I have his back the same way.

Up until my junior year, I had only had one roommate, Demo. Demo and I decided that to save money we would move in with two other male college students our junior year. Of the four roommates, three of us were on football scholarships. For the most part, this arrangement was a great experience. The only issue I had with having one of the new roommates was that he would always throw huge parties. Sounds pretty normal, but the problem was that the parties would be advertised as a "Football Player Party." He would also charge those who attended. This was funny because most times we would not be aware of anything until we arrived home and see about a couple hundred people outside our duplex on any given weekend. The one person in the house that didn't even play football was smart enough to capitalize off of our "status." This particular roommate danced to the beat of a different drum, but he was loyal and had a big heart. He definitely kept things interesting while we lived there, and he was also extremely entertaining.

My other roommate, Jon, played football with us at UNL. Jon is another one of my close friends to this very day, and his family played a major role in Demo and me being comfortable in our new environment. Jon comes from a very large family, right near the university. Their family was very close, and took good care of us every time we visited. His family encouraged us in our faith also. On holidays, they always made sure that my roommates and I knew we were welcome to spend it with them, and treated us like part of the family. Eating with Jon's family at get-togethers was legendary. The food was so amazing, and we would practically eat until we could not move. Thankfully, they would force us take food home too. Being away from home and family wasn't easy at all, but the love of families like this made it a much smoother transition. For them to open up their home without even knowing us was truly a blessing that I am still thankful for.

We became close as roommates and friends during that time together. Another bond that we had was pledging to our fraternities. Eventually, three out of four of us pledged Omega Psi Phi Fraternity Incorporated. The other poor, lonely other roommate decided to pledge Kappa Alpha Psi Fraternity Incorporated, another national historical black fraternity. Take a guess at which roommate would decide to keep it imperfect? I joke around, but sincerely I have no doubt that joining my fraternity was the right decision for me. Joining a Greek- lettered organization is not for everyone, but I think it's a good idea to check it out, keep an open mind and learn about what different organizations stand for and how involved are they in the community.

Let it also be known that for some reason a lot of good memories I have had in my life involve eating. Before I was twenty-one, many of us would go to the downtown Amigos to hang out. Lincoln wasn't as developed back then so there would be a parking lot full of kids eating and hanging out every weekend; at this one in particular since it was downtown. There was a police officer who worked there on the weekends who kept things under control. His name was Mr. Woody and he was a nice guy who really cared about the kids and our safety. He was easy to talk to and always gave great advice to us when we talked to him.

My favorite place to eat in college, The Watering Hole, has by far the best wings in Nebraska. Nowadays, it's much more fancy and family friendly, but back in the day it was a cool dive bar with great food and people. Yia Yia's for pizza, and Ali Baba's for gyros, were also some of my favorite places to eat and pass time. The very first time I ate at Ali Baba's I remember seeing a blackshirt poster on the wall. As I waited for my order, the manager noticed me and pointed at the poster. He said he was a fan and encouraged me to continue to do good and work hard. I never tasted a gyro or even heard of them before coming to Nebraska, but I was hooked right away. Last but not least, Doozy's was my go to for sandwiches in college. I was so sad to see Doozy's close not very long ago! These old staples in Lincoln always bring back great memories of my college years.

Of course, there were so many great moments from the football field as well. I could write a book just about my experiences on the field alone, but there a a few memories that definitely stand out in my mind.

One of my greatest Nebraska memories was receiving my Blackshirt jersey. This was a tradition started by the legendary Husker football coach, Bob Devaney, for his team's first-string defense. I was taught about the tradition of the Blackshirts under one of the greatest defensive coaches in college football, Charlie McBride; about what it means to be able to wear that jersey every day at practice. I learned my freshman year how special it was to be a part of the first-team defense at Nebraska. As a unit, the Blackshirts were an intimidating force. Everyone wanted to be the first one to the ball. It sounded like a call center the way different positions communicated with each other in between plays.

I did not receive my Blackshirt until the end of my freshman year, and when I saw it in my locker I was beyond proud. It was a huge accomplishment so early in my career, and it is still one of my most special ones. I truly learned the pride of becoming a Blackshirt when past players would come share with us their experiences as a Blackshirt, about the tradition of being a Blackshirt, and how proud they were for us to carry on that tradition.

The philosophy is so simple, just as simple as our option offense, as matter of fact. "Beat the man in front of you, use your help, and swarm tackle" are for the most part the "credo" of a Blackshirt. These concepts sound simple, but there is untold work and preparation in achieving these goals. My teammates were very excited for me, and I felt very blessed to be put into a position with that much prestige. A teammate of mine congratulated me and then told me that I would have to work twice as hard to keep it as I did to get it. Those words stuck with me my entire career at Nebraska.

Being a Blackshirt defensive back in particular was challenging but very rewarding. We played different defenses but our primary focus was press-man. Press-man is an aggressive defensive technique that defensive backs use to disrupt the route being run by a receiver during a football play. Learning to have the mentality of shutting down receivers was ingrained into us over the years. I was fortunate enough to learn from some great Nebraska players, and I took full advantage of being under them. We practiced press-man so much, I became better each year as a player and eventually a leader for my team. Being able to effectively play this way made learning other techniques, that I would have to learn at the next level, much less complicated.

To this day being a Blackshirt is a great history that I am grateful to be apart of. Wearing a Blackshirt was an unforgettable experience. Being voted team captain my senior year, and getting my Blackshirt were my favorite memories as a football player in Nebraska.

* * *

There were so many memorable and exciting games I was able to play in during college, but a few definitely stand out, for better or worse.

Early in my college career, we played a game against the University of Southern Mississippi. They were considered a small university but they had a lot of good athletes. That particular year, they had two NFL-caliber receivers and a quarterback with an arm like a cannon. During my week of preparation, I knew this game would be the most difficult challenge for me up to that point in my career, so I studied extra film, and mentally kept my mind on putting myself in a position to be successful on game day. That game was a defensive battle, and we won by a score of 20-13. I had two fourth quarter interceptions to end the game and seal our victory. That game stands out because it gave me the confidence to believe in myself.

KEYUO CRAVER SR.

In a game televised on ABC during my sophomore year, I hit a guy so hard that he was knocked completely out. He played for a school that had recruited me—Texas A&M. I got so many phone calls from family and other people back home who were excited that they had seen me on TV. In one of the reports before the game, one of the Texas A&M coaches who had worked to recruit me said their players were going to pick on the weak link of the defense, which was me, because I was the most inexperienced player on the defensive squad. I was pretty determined to prove him wrong, and I think I did. By the end of the game, I had a few pass breakups, several tackles, and an interception in the fourth quarter. The biggest highlight, however, was knocking that player unconscious on an open field tackle. The legendary Keith Jackson gave the play-by-play with Brent Musburger, and it was a great moment for me — a breakout game. I definitely got the respect of my teammates, coaches and fans afterwards. My family, everybody saw that game. I was becoming somewhat of a playmaker for our team, and it was an awesome feeling.

Those games bring back great memories, but there was one game that was so special I will always cherish that moment. Coming from Texas many would assume that beating UT might be my most memorable game, but my senior year we played against the University of Oklahoma at Memorial Stadium—two great teams with equally talented coaching staffs pitted against each other in one of the greatest rivalries in college football. OU came in ranked #1 in the national polls and we were ranked #2. There was so much hype and media coverage on the game that entire week. As athletes we are taught that every game is the same, but in preparation for this match you knew that there were exceptions to the rule.

The smell of sweat and the high anxiety of the magnitude of this game hung in the air, and one could just see and feel the seriousness on the faces of all the players as we warmed up for the game. There wasn't much talking or dancing around as both teams prepared to play. What a battle and great game! Luckily good faith was on our side, and we prevailed victorious against a great team and one of my favorite college football coaches. Playing in that game truly felt like a dream. It was as if time froze, and it felt so great to be able to experience those few hours on the field. That experience is something many people dream of, and to actually get to live it out is something I will be able to cherish for the rest of my life. I think it's important to note that not all memorable games resulted in us winning and celebrating victory.

The Rose Bowl my senior year was a different story. To this day, that game is still very hard to talk about. Many of my close friends and family still tease me about Andre Johnson. When we first watched film on the team we were to play in the Rose Bowl, and we saw the greatness that was on that squad, everyone looked at me with faces that shouted, "What are we going to do?" I had not been scared of a player since peewee football, but I was nervous — for real.

Andre, in particular, was fast, aggressive and very talented, not to mention the fact that he played with an attitude. In later years, when people would bring up Andre, it bothered me at first, but over time I realized he was a truly special player. If they had to refer to one of the best in order to hurt my ego, I was okay with that.

It's hard to admit, but I know I definitely wasn't as prepared as I should've been to face that team, especially upon realizing that I would be guarding Adrian Peterson at wideout. I had just turned 21, I was traveling with the football team during an exciting bowl season, so as you can imagine I was more attentive to meeting celebrities and being seen in a big and exciting city. Unfortunately, it showed in my performance.

When we were in Beverly Hills for the game, we ran into all kinds of celebrities. My roommate and I caught a cab to the grocery store, and we bumped into Sidney Poitier while he was shopping. The only reason I recognized this prolific actor was because a member of our church used to tell me how much I resemble him. I was too young at the time to realize how much of compliment that was, but as I got older, I was definitely able to be more appreciative of the kind comparison. My roommate and I introduced ourselves to Mr. Poitier and talked with him briefly. He was very nice and kind to speak to us for a few minutes.

During this trip, as our team arrived at our hotel in Beverly Hills from a pracitce, I noticed someone taking pictures near our hotel. I instantly knew who it was because I was from the South and I loved hip-hop music. Master P and his son, Romeo, were standing outside our hotel. A few of my teammates and I approached them to introduce ourselves. I grew up listening to Master P and was excited to meet him. He was very laid back. He talked to us and encouraged us to stay focused and chase our dreams. I find it ironic that I'd eventually get drafted by the New Orleans Saints, and they were from New Orleans. Master P had his publicist get our information, and he and his son took pictures with us. He definitely didn't have to, but they mailed us copies of the pictures they took. I still have those pictures. It was refreshing to meet someone with that status who would make time for us and be so down to earth.

My roommate had a friend who was an MTV VJ. He had gone to high school with her. He said she was going to come and pick my roommate, me, and another teammate up from our hotel and take us out with one of her friends to see the city. I was excited just to see something new, and I wasn't expecting anything other than that. When we got into the car, I was stunned. There was Tatyana Ali driving my roommate and us to a party. I was like, "Ashley Banks from *The Fresh Prince of Bel Air* is taking me out! Wow! What a feeling!"

She was very down to earth, very nice, obviously attractive, very cool, and I just felt like, "You know, I could get used to this." I also met Heather Locklear, Kobe Bryant, and Shaquille O'Neal on that incredible trip. I had pictures taken with all these people, as well. Sadly, my girlfriend at the time was such a jealous person. She found the pictures of me with all of the celebrities and ripped every last one of them up.

Needless to say, that was an exciting trip, but while I was in Beverly Hills, something began to happen to me. I felt myself changing. I started forgetting about the things that got me there. The entire time I was there, I was kickin' it. I forgot about the discipline and the hard work, spending time with myself, and doing the little things that I needed to do to keep myself from being average. I got complacent, and it started showing.

Chapter 4

TO MY FELLOW HUSKERS AND ASPIRING ATHLETES

To college athletes everywhere, but especially to Nebraska Cornhuskers, present and future, I encourage you to not take for granted the short season you have as a student-athlete. One of my biggest regrets is taking that blessing for granted.

It's easy to look back on it and see what I did wrong. I didn't use a lot of the resources that were available to me. I can't tell you how important it is to take full advantage of your resources. Go talk to your counselors and academic advisors. Find ways to sharpen your people skills, network, and explore ways to become more active in your community. These things will have more of an impact for the long term in your life than your actual playing career.

Right now, you're on top of the world, and you think it will last forever, but the truth of the matter is, being an athlete lasts only a short period in your whole life. Yes, it's an amazing experience and definitely a blessing, however, it is just a small window in your life so don't waste time being complacent. Take advantage of that opportunity, take advantage of your resources, get involved in the community, and make as many positive connections as you can.

I regret nothing about my experience at Nebraska, but I also know there were a lot of things I should've done differently. Be mindful of the position you are in and the fact that not everyone has been as fortunate as you. Get out of your comfort zone, and your jam-packed student-athlete schedule, and spend time with people in **underserved communities**—especially with young people who aspire to reach some of the same goals you have reached. This goes such a long way to help and encourage them.

One thing about most universities is that they do a very good job of making sure athletes are taken care of, making sure you have everything you need as far as resources, and helping you stay on task. But, the one thing a university can't do is teach you about your culture or help you get to know yourself.

You get to know yourself by becoming involved in the community. Never get too comfortable or complacent when things seem easy. Don't be fooled by the propaganda that tries to convince you that you as an athlete are superior, invincible, or that nothing can happen to you, because it's not true. I have to admit I was naïve about that, and so I learned a lot of hard lessons.

The university did everything they could do to position me to be successful, but there were just some things I had to do on my own. Because I was immature and not knowledgeable enough, I faced some pitfalls. I encourage athletes to avoid problems like those I created for myself. Give back, really get to know yourself, and it will last a lot longer than what you do on the field of competition.

One of the most lasting and unselfish things you can contribute is the time and attention you give to fans. This is easy to take for granted. From your perspective, you are just going out there and talking to people who see you play. But from their perspective, even a brief contact with you can carry huge meaning, sometimes for the rest of their lives.

I constantly run into kids who were in elementary school back when I played. Now they're grown men, and they still talk about the impact I had volunteering at their school or taking the time to talk with them. As a college kid, I didn't really realize those moments were that important, but when I got older, I realized I wasn't going to be a superstar for the rest of my life and I needed to build something more—something that would last throughout the rest of my days.

The fans in Nebraska are some of the most dedicated, truest fans you will ever meet in your life. When they see you nearby or talk with you, it has a very real impact on them. What an awesome feeling to still meet people to this day who were impacted by me when I was a player. It makes me realize how much of a blessing it was to be there and be able to have an effect on people I didn't even know.

I just thank God that I'm still here and still have a positive attitude—and also the guts to pass on what I've learned. I am able to share what I've been through to those who come after me and who aspire to accomplish some of the same goals I accomplished. I know I won't be able to fix your problems, but at least I hope that I'll get you to be more conscientious of certain decisions. It's up to you to make the right decision in the moment, but I hope you take my advice, as I offer it with the utmost sincerity and with the utmost respect.

I am and always will be a Nebraska Cornhusker. I still bleed Husker Red and still support my univeristy to this day. I thank God I am able to be a part of a legacy that is still unprecedented in college football. I have so much respect for the coaches and support staff who worked with me while I was at Nebraska. Not until I was older did I really realize how much they shaped many of my ideas and my beliefs. I am thankful that I chose to go there.

* * *

It might sound strange, but I don't regret the negative things I have done in my life. Just as I have accepted all the successes, I have had to learn how to accept the failures that I have had in life.

One of my biggest regrets is leaving Nebraska after graduation to go train in Arizona. My agent and I thought it would be best to train out there and get prepared for testing at the NFL combine and for the Senior Bowl. Although I had a lot of fun there, I was definitely not disciplined nor focused, and it affected my performance. It was like I thought I'd already made it to the NFL. All my life I had worked hard for everything I wanted, and then once I knew I was going to the next level, achieving my dreams, I stopped doing the things it took to get there. Rather than take advantage of the resources and facilities I trained at, I was more focused on which nice restaurant I was going to eat at later or how much I would spend at the mall that day. I wanted to show my status before I even had it. As a result of my arrogance and complacency I trained horribly, and tested out terribly at the Senior Bowl and NFL combine. To make matters worse, I got a DUI in Scottsdale Arizona less than a month before the draft.

The day of the Rose Bowl I had around three or four hundred dollars in my checking account. That night, after the game, my agent and I met for dinner. I signed my contract as well a line of credit. The next day when I went to withdraw some cash I noticed over $150,000 in my checking account. I had never seen this much money before so it was definitely a surreal feeling to have access to that much cash. Being so young and inexperienced in life, I felt things would be like this forever.

With no one to educate me on budgeting or investing I went crazy with spending. I spent a lot of money on myself, family, and friends. Over the next few weeks of training I acted as if I had already been in the NFL for several years. Foolishly, it didn't occur to me that I was spending money that I would eventually have to pay back. I spent like I knew that it would be coming in all the time. I wished I would have stayed humble and not taken the money that was offered to me as a line of credit. Before I even signed my professional contract, I owed creditors $150,000 plus interest.

To anyone aspiring to become a professional athlete, one should keep this little nugget in mind: you can't miss what you've never had. Maybe if I would have declined that money up front, things might have played out differently for me—or maybe not. But, my advice for younger athletes in similar situations is this: unless it's a part of your contract, don't take any loans or money before you do your deal. You will have to pay that money back with interest. Most of you come from humble backgrounds, so without proper education about finances, it spells disaster for you. Starting a career in debt without being guaranteed you will make your team's roster could bring you stress that continues into your life for years. Get educated and get a trusted mentor, preferably with previous experience in this unique situation; someone who can offer some financial & lifestyle advice that could make a world of difference for you.

Nonetheless, there I was in Arizona with a lot of money and free time on my hands at the most important time of my life. What was I thinking? That's what I say to myself now as I look back on the many selfish and boneheaded decisions I made. To be real with you, I guess the idea of having freedom sounded preferable to the routine that had been a major part of my life up until that point. I worked out at this training facility for two to three hours a day. The rest of my time was up for me to do whatever I pleased. I ate out a lot, shopped, went to clubs, and didn't really focus on the hard work and discipline that had been my habits that got me to that point.

I was twenty-one years old and I was in a position that most people only dream about. Nobody was around to hold me accountable so I did what felt good and not what I needed to do to put myself in a position to be a successful NFL athlete. I dropped the ball big time, and eventually this behavior and sense of entitlement caught up with me one night in Scottsdale, Arizona.

One beautiful sunny evening as the sun set over the desert horizon, my agent took me and seven or eight other clients out for dinner and drinks in downtown Scottsdale. Beautiful shopping centers, art galleries, and happening bars lined the streets buzzing with busy people out having a good time. That particular night started out great. We ate at an amazing restaurant, laughing and drinking with other men who also had accomplished their dreams of making it to the NFL.

After a couple of hours, everyone started to make plans to leave. But a few of us decided to go out to some nightclubs in the area before ending our night. After going to a few more places and having more drinks, I knew that it was getting late and time for me to get home. I also knew that I was intoxicated, but my ignorance and arrogance got the best of me. Around 2am, as I headed to my car, I had a very uneasy feeling. I didn't even have a chance to pull my car in reverse before a police car was behind me with sirens on.

KEYUO CRAVER SR.

I got arrested for the first time in my life for an "extreme DUI." I was almost two times the legal limit to drive. The officer who arrested me later said that I was so nice and polite that after I was booked, they decided to have an officer drive me home in my car and make sure that I got into my apartment safely. I was so drunk and hung over the next morning that I really thought it was just a bad dream. That wishful thinking quickly vanished as I noticed that I missed about thirty phone calls. Most of them were from my agent, so when I called him back to give him the news I could hear the disappointment in his voice.

Things were quickly going the wrong direction. This incident happened a few weeks before the NFL combine and the Senior Bowl, which is an all-star game for college players. My agents advised me not to mention this incident when I interviewed with teams that wanted to potentially draft me. I was new to this process, so I followed their advice and lied to all the teams that were interested in me. I did so for my own selfish reasons, which eventually would cost me in a catastrophic way. I don't blame the agents I had at the time for that terrible decision I made. I am the one who has to live with the consequences of my actions. It reminded me of the shame I felt when I was a kid and was caught stealing at the store back home in Harleton. Not being forthcoming with the teams was a decision that felt like it would help me take a shortcut, but it actually prolonged the situation more than it helped.

What I didn't know is that every team knew of my DUI, but wanted to see if I had the character to admit my mistake. I had to learn the hard way. Painfully, in their assessments of me, each team questioned my integrity and character. That devastated me. I value both integrity & character so highly and although I know that this wasn't who I was at heart, those teams had every right to feel that way. Adding to these events the poor preparation I took in getting myself ready for the physical testing and drills at the NFL combine, my stock dropped drastically.

As a result of getting an extreme DUI in Scottsdale AZ I was ordered to do fourteen days in the famous "Tent City" jail, where the inmates are dressed in pink socks and sandals. This jail was controlled by Sheriff Joe Arpaio who's known for being tough on people who commit crimes. I must say if anyone who has spent time in jail is comfortable being there, then without a doubt their priorities have definitely fallen out of place. It was such an embarrassing and humbling feeling being in that position.

There I was, two months after being drafted into the NFL, going to serve time for my irresponsible behavior. In that jail, you are treated worse than animals and getting respect was pretty hard to come by. I recall walking through the lunch and TV area when I arrived and immediately being approached by an older African-American who instructed me to go to talk to the person in charge. This man represented the African-Americans in the jail. The "boss" if you will. He let me know how things were run there, where "our" area was to sit, and also which areas to avoid. I calmly thanked him and said that I didn't want any drama, and would do my two weeks and leave.

Serving time in the outdoor jailhouse in the middle of the desert was challenging in itself. 100-degree days and 40-degree nights seemed extreme. I knew to expect blistering heat during the day, but I didn't know it got that cold at night in the desert. The first couple of days being in the desert made time pass too slow for the inmates. After seeing how irritable inmates got due to heat and too much time on their hands, I decided to get a job cooking to pass time. Working that next week made a huge difference and eventually I was able to put that terrible experience behind me. When I was released from the jail I was ready to get away from the state of Arizona. I was ready to just focus on football and going into training camp in great shape. I left the city of Scottsdale within 24 hours of being released from jail.

Don't get me wrong, there were also good experiences during that period, like the week of the Senior Bowl. My trip was really an awesome experience in spite of the trouble I had brought upon myself personally. During that week of practice my draft stock rose again because I competed well all week and proved that I could compete consistently with the best players in the country. After earning a starting spot for my team, during the game I tackled a player, causing me to get a stinger in my neck and shoulder. Since we were all potential high picks for the NFL draft, I was told by medical staff who came out on the field that I had to remain still to be placed on a stretcher. I knew that I wasn't hurt that bad, but I was still forced to do it. The trainers and doctors did an awesome job of making sure that my health and safety were their first concern. I didn't like having to do that or hear it at the time, but I appreciate the way that I was cared for. Maybe that was God's way of letting me know that I wasn't in control, and that I needed to slow things down? Needless to say, I went from a potential first-rounder to hopefully a first day pick, and I was not proud of myself at all.

Chapter 5

From O St. To Bourbon St.

The draft had finally arrived. The weekend of the draft, I decided to drive from Phoenix back to Harleton, TX. I wanted time to myself to reflect on the things that had taken place in my life and also get a game plan together for moving to my next phase in this life process. The ride was so beautiful and peaceful. To ease my mind, I smoked a joint on my drive to Texas. I remember bringing just one with me, because I didn't want another episode with the law. Everything was smooth until I pulled up to the Texas state border, where apparently the patrolmen and his K9-dog could smell the odor of marijuana in my vehicle. While they were questioning me, I remember people looking at my car and at me as they drove through customs. It was pretty embarrassing.

I told the officers that I had just finished training in Arizona to get ready for the NFL draft. I lied, telling them that a few of the guys I trained with and my agent had partied with me the night before, and he possibly smelled smoke due to that. I assured the officers that there was nothing on me or in the car. I consented to a car search and sat as agents talked to me, while other officers and the K-9 went through my belongings. I'm sure they thought I would have drugs in the car with me. They went through my car inside and out, but didn't find anything. During the search, they noticed the Nebraska Cornhusker gear in my trunk and eventually started to understand that I was no criminal. They even asked me for autographs afterward and asked to take pictures with me. As cars passed, now people were looking at me like, "Okay, he must be famous, but who is he?" For the next two to three hours on the highway, I got many honks and waves from other cars that had seen me while passing through the Texas stateline. It was a crazy experience that I know could have turned out a lot worse.

No one in my family knew of all the drama I had been dealing with in Arizona. When I arrived home late that evening, everyone was there, ready to celebrate with me. Family, friends, and church members were all there, and it felt good to have so many come out to support me. Even though I didn't get a call from any teams the first day of the draft, we had a blast eating and talking about all the things it had taken to get to that point. Early the next morning, I got a call from the head coach of the New Orleans Saints at the time, Jim Haslett. Finally, the wait was over, and my lifelong dream had come true. My friend and teammate, Donte Stallworth, who was the first-player drafted to the Saints that year, also called to congratulate me. We had played against each other in college and had tremendous respect for one another on the football field. It was happening! I was actually living my childhood dream. I was officially a professional athlete.

* * *

I really can't put into words the level of anxiety one goes through going into their first training camp in the NFL. That type of pressure is not for the faint of heart. The New Orleans Saints training camp was held in Thibodaux, Louisiana. I was there for business, so I didn't get to take it all in, but I did notice that it was swampy, humid, and full of very nice people who were crazy about their New Orleans Saints.

It was a blessing that I was still able to get drafted by the New Orleans Saints, and I didn't take it for granted. I was just relieved to finally be able to say that had I accomplished my lifelong dream of becoming a professional football player. I decided to go back to Nebraska over the summer to work out with my former teammates at the college where I had built a great reputation, and had put in great summer workouts before. I trained hard and got myself in the best shape possible.

It definitely showed on the field as well. I was focused and fluid, and during training camp I quickly caught my coaches' attention as to the type of player I could be when I was on top of my game. I was one of the best defensive backs in the entire camp. I got a lot of praises, and I really began to believe in myself again. I saw that being a professional football player was something I could definitely succeed at. It felt good to get the notoriety and attention again. As long as I was in shape, focused, and staying out of trouble, I was doing what I needed to do.

With the setback of the DUI, I was put into the NFL's substance abuse program. This gave them the right to test me and put me through evaluations for my first two years in the league. Initially, I didn't see it as a problem. I was just happy to be in the NFL.

I have to say, the experience was just so surreal. It was quite an honor to go from growing up, watching some of my favorite football players—such as Joe Horn, Dale Carter, and Norman Hand (RIP)—to now being side-by-side with these men as teammates. It felt like a solid accomplishment.

Some people don't know that Mike Riley, later head coach of the Nebraska Cornhuskers, was my position coach during my rookie year with the Saints. I didn't know much about him, but it didn't take long to see that he was one of the nicest people you will ever meet. I was so young and immature, but he told me that I had a lot of talent and potential, and believed I could play a very long time in the NFL.

Coach Riley was an offensive-minded coach, and I played defense, but he knew football and made learning the game simple. His laid-back approach definitely made me go into practices and games in a more relaxed state of mind. During a time when everything around me was so fast-paced and stressful, I respected that calm, relaxed aura he had about himself. Fast-forward fifteen years later and he was our beloved coach at UNL. When he was first announced as head coach, I knew he would be a great fit. I assured several faithful Nebraska fans that he was a great coach and a man of integrity.

There are so many small, happy moments I remember whenever I think back to that first training camp—such as arriving on the football field early to catch punts from our kickers and watching the equipment managers trying to get alligators off our practice field. But I could still feel the stress of some of the most intense moments of my life pulling at me. If you ever find yourself in a similar key place in life, please try your best to surround yourself, especially in your personal life, with positive, supportive people who can spur you on forward towards your goals. You make much better decisions from a peaceful place. Even if you know it will not be easy, having more balance in your life will help you accomplish your dreams— be it the prestigious honor of making it onto an NFL roster or meeting whatever goal you are trying to accomplish.

* * *

When I was in training camp, one woman in particular was in my life that reaped the benefits of being with a professional athlete. I am sorry to say that a lot of people in my life at the time did not support me positively or uplift me the slightest bit, and this woman was no different. I have no one to blame for this but myself, and I hope that some young man or young woman can learn from my mistakes, so they don't have to go through what I went through.

I remember I had just finished training camp my rookie year, and my parents who I hadn't seen since I was drafted drove my girlfriend at the time across several states to move in with me. I wrote my parents a $10,000 to thank them for everything they had done for me as parents, and also for going out of their way to make me happy. I thought nothing of the gesture and was so happy about their excitement when they took it. We didn't have a lot of money growing up, but I was a super happy kid and always knew both of my parents loved my brothers and me unconditionally.

The woman I was dating at the time heard the excitement and came downstairs, asking what all the commotion was about. She then saw the check my mother put down onto the table, and she went to look at it. After reading the check, the first thing that came out of her mouth was, "What the hell did you do that for?" I really thought she was joking, but quickly realized this indeed was not a joke. She then told my parents they were horrible, deadbeat parents, and she hoped I didn't grow up to be terrible like them. I had never heard someone, especially my age, talking about my parents like that, or disrespecting them directly. I guess, if she really felt that way, there's nothing I can do about that. Everyone has the right to feel what they feel, but it was wrong of her not to talk with me privately about it, rather than insulting them and putting us all in that awkward predicament.

I was deeply hurt and embarrassed. Here was this woman that I thought wanted to be with me, who had been living off me for the previous couple of years, paying no bills but spending my money, with the nerve to judge the very people who opened their home to her and sacrificed their time to make me happy. I wanted her to be a part of my life, but I began to see there was absolutely no way that was going to happen.

My parents were in shock. We tried to leave the hostile environment, but my girlfriend grabbed and hid my car keys and gate opener to the apartment complex, preventing us from leaving. Never in my life before, or since, have I had to deal with that much hatred coming my way, and I thank God no one was hurt at the time. We could only just sit there and listen to her continue to disrespect my family and me. The verbal abuse finally stopped, but none of us slept much that night.

Unfortunately, that incident wasn't the first clue I'd had that something was wrong in the relationship. Just two weeks earlier, my best friend had given me a call while I was in training camp, telling me that he had run into her at a club with another man—and my dumb ass still tried to salvage this very toxic relationship.

After the episode with my parents and the check, I called my girlfriend's parents right away and explained to them why they should come get their daughter. She didn't have a way home, and I made it clear to them that it was time for her to go. I had to go to practice the next morning, leaving my parents with her while we waited for her parents to drive from another state to take her home.

By the time I got home from practice, just my mom and dad were at the house. We had a discussion for several hours about the relationship, the events leading up to the main event, and how to approach things moving forward. For the first time, my parents shared that they never thought it was a wise decision to date her. I asked why they never mentioned it to me before, and they said they wanted to support my decisions and not interfere with whoever I decided to be with.

When you think you are in love, you overlook the obvious. It was as if a ton of bricks had fallen on me. The entire relationship passed before my eyes and I realized none of it was real. This person never supported or encouraged me, and I allowed her to be my partner during some of the most pivotal years in my life. On the other hand, I can't fully blame her. She, too, was just a young kid trying to figure life out and being young, selfish, and immature myself didn't help either. At that time I questioned why did I have to learn such a harsh and difficult lesson like this at that stage in my life but as I got older I realized our trials are the way we gain wisdom.

Years later, in looking back at my relationships, I really started to question what was my drive in wanting to stay in some of them? I could never understand why some of my girlfriends could take so much from me, but still treat me hatefully. So many times, women have tried to provoke me to do things that could have jeopardized my future and my career. It used to surprise me at the lengths a person would go in order to destroy you if they really want something. Thank You, Jesus, for giving me restraint at those times, so I never fell for that trap by doing something foolish that would have cost me my freedom. I'll be the first to admit I could have done a lot of things differently. I made some bad decisions, but I can only accept my faults and try to be better. The lesson in all this for my fellow athletes (or any man or woman in a situation such as this)? Please remove yourself from this environment, because nothing positive will come of it when emotions are running high. Make sure whoever you choose to be with in life not only respects you, but also respects your family and where you came from. I know that two people in any relationship can and will see things differently, but without mutual respect and understanding it would be hard for any relationship to grow.

* * *

When you are a rookie, the veterans like to do little things to push you around in fun. The Saints veterans made us do things like sing during lunch or downtime. Occasionally, some first-year players had to take the

I PEED & FORGOT

older players' pads to the locker room, but it never got more serious than that. Humility goes a long way, and I think it was just a way to check us younger players' egos.

When a rookie couldn't humble himself and refused a veteran's request, it brought much heat and unwanted attention to that athlete. Even if you are not used to being humble, football is a team sport, and being able to show that you're all about the team can save you a lot of drama. Humbling yourself early may eventually pay off in a major way.

Here's my rookie advice: Don't make it all about you. Don't take those rookie duties so personally. You are not the first, and you are definitely not the last to go through things like that. Think of it as a good thing. Once things are looking good for a player as far as their chances of making it on the team, when training camp is coming to an end, that's when the practical jokes start. You begin to see your teammates' true personalities coming out, as well as the coaches'. It's such a great feeling of accomplishment and a sense of finally belonging when one gets to that point, a few playful veterans' demands can't take that away.

My first training camp was by far my most positive one, and I learned a lot about myself along that journey. In my next two training camps, things were different. I wish I had it to do over again, but as with everything else that happened to me, all I could do is learn from my mistakes. I didn't prepare myself physically or mentally for what I was going to endure in those following two camps, and that is why my career was cut so short.

How could I have done it differently? Stay humble and disciplined. Stay motivated and focused, so you can give yourself the best possible chance of accomplishing an almost-impossible dream. This applies not only in sports but in any endeavor in life. I worked most of my life to watch it disappear within a fraction of that time it took to get there. Don't take this precious opportunity for granted!

When I arrived in New Orleans to begin playing for the Saints, there was a lot to enjoy—and a lot to lose. I remember when the first car I ever bought as a professional athlete was delivered to me in New Orleans. It was a 2002 Lexus LS 430 and I thought I was a boss for sure. That status of being an

NFL player is such a wonderful feeling, and I was so grateful because God promised me if I sacrificed that he would get me here. So much about the city was exciting and new for me. I felt on top of the world. New Orleans is a city unlike any other.

It was, of course, a big adjustment for an East Texas country boy. There I was, drafted into Who Dat Nation in New Orleans, a very fast-paced and diverse big city, coming from small conservative Nebraksa city. I met a lot of good people in New Orleans, and ate some of the best food I've ever eaten in my life. Some of my favorite restaurants to this day—Dragos, Two Sisters, and The Wing Shack—are all places where I really loved eating when I did my time there in New Orleans.

The culture of "The Big Easy" was colorful and eye-opening. I learned things I never would have guessed. When I first arrived as a rookie, they took us through an orientation designed to help us adjust to the new living environment and city. During this time, the players learn a lot about the city, the people, and also about certain places in the city that could potentially be dangerous when there at the wrong time. One topic in particular that was discussed was definitely a bit surprising to me. They explained some of the strange things that could happen in NOLA, and that players should be careful when meeting some women in the city who might actually be men. Apparently, there were men who really looked like women and they had no problem leading people onto believe they were women. We were taught some "warning signs" to look for. Coming from a small town and having spent the previous few years of my life in the small city of Lincoln, Nebraska, I really had to think about that.

I had been seeing a young, light-skinned lady who I was just beginning to talk on the phone with regularly, and I was never worried about getting to know her. She was slim, pretty, very sweet, and down to earth. I even surprised myself when I actually took the time to approach her, and eventually ask for her phone number. Her New Orleans accent was attractive to me, and I was excited to know her.

It was during this same time period that I started taking the orientation regarding cross-dressers. What took the cake for me was when one of the veterans on the team told me about an experience he had when he first came to New Orleans. He said that within the first few months of being in the city, he met a girl he liked that was smart, and also very cute to him. After talking a few times, he asked her out. From the beginning, he said that they both hit it off very well. He said he noticed that she took things slow, and for him that was good because he wasn't used to that. And then one night while on a date, the two decided to go to her apartment and have a couple drinks before they called it a night. The evening was going so well, they eventually ended up kissing. He said that as they kissed something didn't feel right. He said it was weird because this woman was the "strongest kisser" he had ever met. I left that alone, but when he followed that with, "Her jaws were powerful," I spit my drink out I was laughing so hard.

The story continued and the woman started crying and said that they needed to talk. My teammate was nervous because he had no clue what was to be expected. He asked what was wrong, and the person explained how she didn't know she would like him so much, but before they continued to talk it was important to tell him something. My friend was trying to be patient, but it was definitely wearing thin. "Please don't be upset," is what the person said next. By now my friend is visibly frustrated and asks, "Please tell me what you have to say."

"I'm a man!" she screamed out, "I wanted to tell you sooner but..." Listening to the story, I couldn't contain myself. I was like, "But? But what?!" He said "but" was the last word he heard as he ran out of the apartment door. Needless to say, this scared the you know what out of me! After hearing all of this I felt a bit overwhelmed.

I am ashamed to say, I was spooked. I stopped talking with the lady I had met. I'd like to apologize right now to the lovely person that I was too scared to take a chance to get to know a little better because of my own insecurities. If by chance you are reading this, I want you to know that you were really sweet, but I was too traumatized to find out if the same thing was going to happened to me.

Back on the field, I had a successful rookie year, playing very well, and doing a lot of great things. Some of my childhood idols even complimented me on my playing in the first year. I felt like that was the way it was supposed to be. I felt like it would be that way forever. But I was a young kid who didn't know any better. Playing football was easy. The hardest part for me about playing as a professional athlete was staying focused away from the field, and I later fell into the traps of success. I was young, black, and successful— it made me a target.

Unthinkable challenges in my personal life added to my inability to focus after the first year. One of the most difficult experiences I had to deal with as a young professional football player was my baby daughter's serious illness. I found out not long after the year ended that my daughter, Rayn, was in the hospital and would have to undergo brain surgery to remove a tumor. She wasn't even a year old and had a tumor the size of a golf ball in her head.

It was hard to focus on football and training while my little girl was suffering. She was so strong through that ordeal. I couldn't imagine how a person so young could be so resilient. I knew from the beginning that Rayn was special, but to see her recover so well from something so traumatic was nothing less than a miracle. Even as a little bitty thing, her attitude and personality through that situation was inspiring. But, for me it was one of the scariest things I have ever had to deal with. I thank God that she was able to recover fully from that tumor, and I know she will achieve great goals in life. She has been special since birth, and I believe her recovery is proof that God has shown her favor.

Despite that scary time in my personal life, on the field, things were going great. I was almost ready to be a full-time starter. I found myself in a game against the Green Bay Packers, playing against Brett Favre, another of my childhood heroes, and I played the game of my life, including scoring a touchdown. But with about three minutes left in the game, I made a tackle and heard my knee snap and went down hard. Brett told me to get up and then told me I had played a great game, so I really, really tried to get back on my feet, but it was too painful. What a surreal feeling to hear one of my childhood idols give me a great compliment, only to have it followed by being taken off the field on a cart with a torn MCL and PCL.

That was when everything changed for me. I was no longer an asset, and no one knew how long I'd be out. Not only did I get no attention from my coaches, but my fellow players, my teammates, and other staff also seemed

I PEED & FORGOT

to shun me. There were a lot of factors that began to spell out more trouble: I had a lot of time on my hands. I wasn't traveling with the team. I wasn't practicing. I was just rehabbing.

Until that time, I had no regular habits of going out, or drinking, nor with smoking, but then I got complacent. I became careless and began feeling entitled and getting too prideful. With too much time on my hands, I started going out to the clubs, at first only once a week, and then it went to twice a week. Eventually, I graduated to going out almost every night.

I wasn't smoking a lot of weed, but I was drinking heavily after a few weeks following the injury. I found myself trying to manipulate the system. I knew I would get random drug tests, but I still went out partying and drinking a lot. I started failing drug tests for alcohol, not really understanding the consequences, and not fully taking advantage of the resources I had available. There were people I could have confided in who maybe could have helped me. Instead, I turned to alcohol and partying where people who knew I was a professional football player would tell me anything that I wanted to hear, build my confidence up, and build my ego up. I let it happen, all the while knowing they didn't care about me.

I made friends with locals in the city who eventually ended up robbing me while I was away visiting my daughter. I came home from a trip to Nebraska, and my car looked like a spaceship, with no rims or tires. The only people who knew I was out of town that weekend had been my girlfriend at the time and another local friend. Another time, a $7,000 necklace was stolen from me while my car was getting washed around that same particular friend so I had to wise up and fast. All that time, I was trying to prove to these "friends" that I was down to earth and humble, and all the while I was getting taken advantage of and plotted against.

I recently spoke with one of my former teammates with the Saints, who actually was born and raised in New Orleans. As we talked and caught up on life, we reminisced about our playing days. I opened up to him about the things I had been doing and how I wasn't focused in those days. He mentioned that he knew a lot about what I was doing back then because he knew a lot of the guys I was hanging around. He also told me local thugs in the city that ran in the same circle as me had talked about setting me up or robbing me. It's crazy to know those things are being contemplated by people you just wanted to be on the same level with.

That life was a gift, and it makes me feel sick that I took it for granted all that time by losing myself in alcohol, drugs, and partying. When I failed my third drug test, I got suspended from the NFL. As you can imagine, it was a very, very tough moment in my life. I had never dealt with that type of adversity. I isolated myself and that made things worse for me. Eventually I failed another drug test and was suspended for a full season. I tried my best to blame everyone but myself even though I knew it was me who had turned my back on them.

While I was playing, I met famous people and experienced red-carpet treatment at restaurants and clubs. I had the opportunity to watch the Final Four basketball tournament at our stadium, and actors, such as Jamie Foxx, crashed our party and hung out with us at our suite. It was a great feeling to rub shoulders with such successful people. And I lost all of it. Because I wasn't focused enough on my craft, this dream was very short-lived.

I truly believe that if I would have stayed focused on what it took to get there and not so much on the people surrounding me who only served to build up my ego, I could probably still be playing to this day. On the other hand, I'm thankful for the lessons I've learned despite all the setbacks. I can't deny that having to face all those issues made me a stronger, smarter, better person than I probably would have ever thought to be. In the midst of these storms there was a rainbow given to me with the birth of my son Keyuo Jr in early 2005. He looks just like his mother but he acts so much like me it's extremely easy being his dad. I know what he is doing before he does it and why! It's like I can read his mind, and can't help but laugh because he does remind me a lot of myself. My kids definitely were able to lift me up during some of the most darkest days of my life.

In the end, my league experience was definitely what some say the NFL stands for: Not for Long. I played two years as a professional player and was suspended in my third year. As talented as I was, I wasn't able to make my way back.

It was a huge loss for me in so many ways. Playing for the New Orleans Saints was fun. They have some of the craziest, most dedicated fans you will ever meet. They're very enthusiastic, loyal, and passionate—a lot like the passion fans in my hometown have for their high school football team, and the beloved fans in Nebraska. The Saints didn't have a whole lot of history with winning, but the culture was rich, and the loyalty was deep, and the fans were straight up and didn't hold anything back—very real and very honest.

I felt a big hole in my life when I had to leave the Saints—and it made me sick to think I lost it for reasons that were in my control. I just wasn't focused. I was young, and I was extremely immature. Oh yea, can't forget arrogant also. But most of all I was selfish, and it showed in my behavior and in my actions. Of course, everybody would love to get a second chance to not make the same mistakes if they could. But now I thank God for the blessings of all those experiences, for bringing me through it, and allowing me to learn some very valuable lessons that will carry over until I die.

* * *

Google made everything worse, because this all happened during the start of the tech boom. I wish I had thought of that when I was choosing to start making those terrible choices.

When I got suspended from the NFL, it was about the time Google's search engine became popular, and looking people up was easy. People could type in your name and both good and bad information would come up. It was a little intimidating when strangers came up to me and told me things they knew about me. One day, I was talking to a clinician provided by the NFL, and he mentioned the possibility of me being suspended for a year if I failed another drug test. I was surprised he knew, and then he told me he had seen it on Google. I knew all of that, and I realized people would be able to look me up, but I still didn't take my situation seriously. I minimized what I was up against, in part because I was being arrogant.

Arrogance kept me from opening up and confiding in anybody, including my closest family and friends. I was getting calls from league officials to talk about my situation, too, but I ignored them. Arrogance allowed me to continue doing what I wanted and not think about the consequences.

When I found out I would be suspended for a year, I didn't believe it was actually happening. Reality quickly set in when I was watching ESPN one morning. In bold letters, it showed: "NFL defensive back Keyuo Craver of the New Orleans Saints suspended for violating league's substance abuse policy."

I hit rock bottom. I literally wanted to crawl up under a rock and die. I started receiving numerous phone calls about what was happening, but didn't know how to handle it. I hadn't even told my parents what was happening. For many of my close friends and relatives, it was the first they heard about what I was facing. It was embarrassing. It was by far one of the hardest things I've had to deal with in my life and the lowest rock bottom I had ever endured. League officials, coaches, clinicians and I were all told before the next training camp that I had failed my last drug test and would not be allowed to play for a year. But I was allowed to attend the 2004 training camp anyway, and I guess the suspension didn't seem real until I saw it on national tv. I was in denial the entire time, until I realized I was being taken out of the the game plan and off of certain positions as we prepared for a preseason game. And then it became real.

I wasn't prepared for this at all, and my lack of maturity was starting to catch up with me. I thought, "Where in the hell did all of my friends and associates go?" It was a very low point in my life, and I hadn't been through anything as serious as this. There is no way to mentally prepare myself for the hardships that lay ahead. One thing I knew I would not do was blame others for my misfortune. If I could take the credit so easily when good things happened, then I had to learn to take the responsibility for the bad as well.

Luckily for me, my parents were in town during training camp that year, because they knew I was dealing with adversity, but they didn't know the extent of everything. I hadn't told them because I thought I could handle it on my own. If it hadn't been for them, I don't know how I would've made it through that agonizing time. Not only was I facing the suspension, but I was going through a breakup with my fiancée. When it rains it pours, and boy was I in need of a king-sized umbrella.

When I finally broke the news to my parents that I would be suspended for a year, I felt mortified explaining it to them. I love them so much, and didn't want to hurt them or let them down. To their credit, they didn't judge me at all. They let me know they were there to support me and encouraged me to work on getting myself where I needed to be. As I said, having them there helped me out tremendously. Their comfort, mom's cooking, and just knowing I still had them there made a big difference in my attitude. I'm sure I was dealing with depression at that time, but my parents' presence made me feel much better. It had taken my whole life to accomplish this dream, but only three years to lose it. I was left wondering what to do next with my life.

My life changed drastically after that. It allowed me to see how many people I had in my life for the wrong reasons. Some people who I had considered my closest friends stopped answering my phone calls. Women I was close to ignored me, as well. People who had benefited from me being a professional athlete talked about me behind my back. They didn't show any sympathy or give any encouragement while I was at the lowest I had been in my life. I hold no grudges and feel no animosity toward any of them, but it was such a tough pill to swallow when I thought those people would be loyal to me until the end. As a matter of fact, it was the opposite.

Some of my biggest supporters when I was in my glory days became my toughest critics when I hit rock bottom. When I returned to Nebraska for a brief period, one of my fraternity brothers mentioned to me that a well-respected member of our organization was telling other members I was out partying and snorting cocaine all night on multiple occasions. Granted, I was doing a lot of things I had no business doing, but that wasn't ever one of them. I felt bad, because it was so far from the truth, but I learned that many people actually would rather believe a lie than accept the truth.

Dealing with this taught me how to focus more on being true to myself and not try to go out of my way to please others. It's truly taken years to get myself back together and focused on becoming a better version of Keyuo. Most people in life can mask or hide from their demons, but going through this in public allowed me to get real with myself and understand where I had failed as an athlete and as a person.

Even during those dark times, I always kept a close relationship with God. I stayed prayed up. I always found a way to go to church and at least try to find some peace there. When I was dealing with that rock bottom in my life, I felt a burning need to get closer to God and to my family, so I proposed to the girl I was dating at the time. I really thought we had a strong bond, a strong connection. She said yes.

A few days before the wedding, my family and best friends were in town. My bride called me, my parents, and her mom into a room and told us she didn't want to go through with the wedding. I was heartbroken, but my daddy said I was the luckiest man in the world. At the time, I didn't know what he meant by that, but he was absolutely right. You shouldn't marry someone just to get married. You should plan on settling down with the person who's your best friend, a person who wants to grow with you, a person who wants to work with you and struggle with you. As much as it hurt, it ended up being a blessing in disguise.

Despite the negativity surrounding us doing this time, we still managed to have a beautiful healthy son together. He was such a blessing for me mentally and spiritually. Though he was born in the midst of such a difficult season of setbacks and shortcomings in my life, his birth really helped me through the most challenging part of my life until that point. I was able to focus my energy more on his happiness and less on my depressing situation. There was no way I could forget what I was dealing with, but being able to hold my son made enduring stress more manageable. Jr. (Keyuo) is such an energetic and competitive kid, and will talk anyone's head off who will listen. A far different tune than how he was as as a toddler who didn't want anyone holding him except his mother or father.

I was out of football for a year and didn't know if I even wanted to continue playing, However I soon got a call from a team in the CFL which is the Canadian Football League. I was asked if I was interested in playing for the Edmonton Eskimos in Edmonton Alberta, Canada. I didn't know much about Canada or the CFL, and I knew even less about the Edmonton Eskimos, but I was very interested. I saw it as a fresh opportunity to compete at a sport I still loved and was good at playing. Despite certain choices I had made, football had done so much for me. After facing a rock bottom and a broken heart, I decided to become an Edmonton Eskimo, and moved to Canada.

Chapter 6

OH, CANADA!

When I got off the plane in Edmonton, I could smell the difference in the air immediately. My breathing was just so much better due to being so far up north. So right off the top, I was in love with my new environment. How could I not love fresh, clean air, and a fresh start. For the first time in a long time, I was clear-headed and determined to take advantage of the opportunity I had being in a new environment.

After all I had been through the first few years following college and as a professional football player, I was ready for a change. I loved football, and was really grateful I had been given another chance to play. Edmonton Eskimos was a storied program, and my first training camp in the CFL was quite an experience.

I learned quickly that playing in the CFL is a big privilege. Team spots are competitive and the sport up there is extremely competitive. Teams can have only a certain number of Americans, and a lot of people were vying to be one of the Americans chosen for their team. Fortunately, I was good enough to make the team there my first year, but I wasn't good enough to play right away, so I had to watch a lot from the sideline. I spent time in a familiar and satisfying routine: working out, staying focused, and getting back in great shape.

Some of the basics of living in Canada took getting used to. Training camp was held at the University of Alberta, which was a beautiful campus right

I PEED & FORGOT

in the city of Edmonton. One day, after the last of two practices in training camp, I fell asleep in my room around 7:30 p.m. When I woke up, it was full sunlight outside with birds chirping. I immediately assumed I had overslept and was late for practice, so I panicked and started rushing to get my clothes on and go to practice. I knew if I was late, it could cost me an opportunity to play for this awesome organization.

I rushed out of my room, ran into the hall and headed for the locker room, but I noticed my teammates were in the conference room where the players lounged and watched TV. Still in a state of panic, I said, "Are we finished with the first practice already?" They all looked just as puzzled and confused as me. Finally, one of my teammates, calling me by my nickname, said, "Crave, you do realize it's just 10:30 p.m.?" I was baffled. It didn't even attempt to get dark up there until 11:00 p.m.

I was so relieved, but I did not feel smart at that moment, and I was a little worried about adjusting. There were a lot of veterans on the team who were not really open to younger guys coming in and taking their spots. It took a while for my roommate and I to gain the respect of our teammates. Therefore, in our first few weeks, we felt like we were on our own.

One night, when my roommate and I were out eating, we met a group of guys from the Middle East—Pakistan, Iraq, and Lebanon. They could tell we were from America, and they befriended us. We got to know one another pretty well and spent a lot of time with them. They welcomed us as if we were family into their homes, and we considered them our first family in Edmonton. Whatever we needed, they helped us get. If we needed to go somewhere or needed to know about anything, they helped us out. They became our brothers, ranking even before our football brothers. It seemed odd, because I didn't know anything about these guys or where they came from.

As we became closer friends, I learned a lot about certain Middle Eastern cultures and about their beliefs. They were Muslims, and they taught us a lot about how they were raised, how they view Americans, and how they view Christians. It was very interesting. We were able to talk about our differences in a constructive manner. They felt strongly about some of their beliefs, and my roommate and I felt strongly about some of our beliefs, but we still showed one another a lot of respect.

When we would see beautiful women (because there were definitely a lot of beautiful women in Canada) they would call them out, but if we saw a beautiful woman from their country and we called them out, they would get extremely upset and offended. They criticized us for being "American" and not holding our tongues and for all we stand for. Then we would have to call them hypocritical. It was all in fun, and nobody ever got too serious. Even though some of our views were different, we were able to communicate openly with them and remain close friends. Even to this day I still call them close friends and talk to them as well.

* * *

Despite the lonliness on the team initially, it still felt great being part of the Edmonton Eskimos. It was a historic team with great fans in a great city. And, in a lot of ways, my horizons expanded while I was there. For example, my passion for hockey grew while I was in Edmonton. Hockey is to Canada what American football is to the United States. I watched some great hockey players and teams and learned a lot about their sport. It was a refreshing change from what I was used to.

I also met a beautiful lady there and we got very close. We fell in love, and eventually had a child together. Being a professional athlete is hard work and time-consuming, and it takes a lot of sacrifice. Being a family man at the same time can feel impossible. I was only there for six months of the year, then would go home to the States for six months, and a lot can happen in that time. We faced many challenges, and I'm sorry it ended. But we still have a beautiful son, Issa—a gorgeous, smart, intelligent kid who is growing fast, and is very, very bright.

Issa is also a fast runner, and I know where he gets it from. I remember the very first date his mother and I went on together. We went to dinner and a movie. As we were leaving the movie theater, she challenged me to a foot race. Initially I thought she was joking, but she was definitely serious. Up until that moment on the date, she had been a quiet, reserved, and shy woman, but as we took our marks to race, her face got really serious. I noticed it, but didn't think anything of it.

I called off the start, and I couldn't believe how fast she was. After three or four steps, I thought, "There is no way I'm going to get embarrassed like this on a first date," and I literally stopped running and started walking. It surprised me, and I respect her for that speed! At least it was passed down to our son.

In my rookie year with the CFL, I didn't see playing time in an actual game until a little more than halfway through the season. There was an injury in the defensive backfield, at one of the positions I played, and so I was the next man up. I was in the best shape of my life, so I was ready for this opportunity. After that game, we went on a winning streak, made it to the playoffs, won two road games in the playoffs, and then played in the Grey Cup, which is like the NFL's Super Bowl. I started my rookie year in the biggest game in Canada against a really good team, and we won.

I played a pretty good game, and winning obviously felt great! Can you imagine what a good feeling it was after all I'd been through? I hadn't felt that much success on the field for a couple of years. Although I wasn't making the same money as in the NFL, I still was able to bring home a good piece of change.

My first year in the CFL was one of my best life experiences, but the hardest thing I had to deal with was not being able to see Keyuo Jr. regularly. I was not able to see my son for almost six months. His mother and some of her family members would always be sure to remind me when we talked on the phone that Keyuo Jr. would not remember me. Being away from your child for six months is a terrible feeling, but I knew my bond with my son was strong. When I finally returned home after the season, my son's mother picked me up from the airport and was kind enough to remind me again that my son probably would not recognize me. When we arrived at her mother's home where everyone was gathering, I walked straight to my son. I took a knee and reached my arms out to him. The house was packed with both adults and kids. It was so quiet you could hear a mosquito burp in the room. It felt like everyone was looking at us, and just like I knew he would, Keyuo opened his arms and walked straight to me! He knew exactly who I was. His mother gave me the most disgusted look, and I couldn't have been more proud as a dad.

After winning the Grey Cup in 2005, I really felt like I was coming into my own again as an athlete, but there's the problem: success. One thing I have learned about success is that you have to manage it. You have to be able to handle it, or it will handle you. I was still just a young dude, and once again I just wasn't as prepared and focused as I should have been. I would climb a mountain and, instead of getting ready to climb another one, I would relish in the moment, pat myself on the back, and let people in who wanted to enjoy the moment with me, but didn't want to help me to go to the next phase in my life.

Then one of the worst things happened. My grandmother, my Madear, the one person I loved and respected the most, the woman who raised me, the one who protected me from harm and put up with my childhood pranks, was suddenly gone. I'd like to say I handled it well, but the truth is that I did not. Add that to the pressures of success that were swirling around me again, and it was a recipe for disaster.

Death affects so many people on different levels. I have lost classmates, associates, and friends, but when my grandmother passed away in 2006, it had a lasting impact on me. Up until her death, I had never experienced the death of a very close relative. When I got word of her passing, I was living and training in Canada, getting ready for the upcoming football season. I remember the phone call from my aunt and what I felt like the instant she delivered the news. There is no way to prepare for the death of a loved one, but when it takes you by surprise it will take your feet out from under you. I remember screaming and crying because I knew I wouldn't be able to see her ever gain. I had lost forever the person who had done more than I can express for me and taught me so much in life. I regret that I wasn't able to tell her how much she meant to me before she was gone.

Our family had been so close, but after she passed greed and deceit entered our lost family and divided some of us. After that experience, I want my kids, nieces, and nephews to know the value of true love in a family and the lack of real value in worldly possessions. There was a time when material things were important to me, but I realized that once you die, none of that matters anymore.

Don't get me wrong, I want my family to have the best out of life, but not at the expense of happiness or true love within my family. My brothers and I keep in very close communication with one another, and we are trying to make sure that the divisions that happened after my grandmother's passing will not happen again. It's about love and family having one another's back, and we intend to make sure our younger generation understands that.

My grandmother's death was so painful, I didn't know what to do with myself. I wallowed in complacency again. I did not have a good off-season before my second year in the CFL. I ended up switching positions. One of my biggest regrets as a football player in the Canadian Football League was that I moved from the corner position to a halfback position, and I really think that hurt my career.

In one game in 2006, we were playing against a guy who was basically the Jerry Rice of the CFL: Milt Stegall. Our squad played a great game against him. We shut him down. I, in particular, had a great game covering him. With an interception, I held him under a hundred yards receiving. The game was less than ten seconds away from being over. We had them deep in their territory. We ran a safety blitz to apply some pressure, and with no safety help Milt Stegall beat me on the last play of a football game for a one-hundred-yard touchdown pass. To this day, I hate the word "fido," because it was our coverage call on that play. It was such a kick in the gut—one of the lowest points in my CFL playing career by far.

I like thinking about the great players I had the privilege of playing against in Canada and in the U.S. Andre Johnson, who I mentioned earlier, was probably the hardest receiver I have ever had to cover. I also had a chance to play against that great Miami team loaded with so many NFL caliber athletes, and the eventual 2002 National Champions. (RIP Sean Taylor). There was even an NFL Hall of Famer on that squad. I also played against Ricky Williams, a Heisman Trophy winner from University of Texas my freshman year at UNL. He was definitely a man amongst boys. And I can't forget how awesome it was to actually play alongside a Heisman Trophy Winner, my former teammate and friend Eric Crouch. He was as humble as they come, but boy was he lethal on the field. A defensive players best friend, IF you were on the same team!

In 2006, not consoling myself with the fact that he was a legend, after handing Milt Stegall that touchdown, I was pretty much ready to go back to the States. I felt like I was hated by the coach, and I was not at a good place in my life or in a good place mentally as a football player. I was getting beat up by the media. It was really hard for the coaches to have faith in me, and it was a very trying time for me as an athlete.

I got benched and had to watch my brothers play from the sideline. I was twenty-five and for the first time in my life I started to seriously think about what I wanted for myself after football. I knew I still had a lot of years of playing in me, but I began to realize that window was closing very fast.

We had a terrible season that year in Edmonton, and I was on the cusp of getting cut from the football team. That year, we ended up 3–13, coming off a Grey Cup championship the year before. It was a huge contrast, but also typical in the life of a professional athlete.

I was still under contract, but rather than honoring my contract and coming back to Canada for the next year, I decided to stay in the States. In spite of my previous bad experiences in Arizona, I moved back to that state and decided to play Arena Football for the Arizona Rattlers. I went from the big playing field of the CFL to a small arena style game, which has a very quick pace, a completely different style of football.

When I look back, I believe I was fortunate to play in three very different leagues: the NFL, the CFL, and the Arena Football League. I learned football points and philosophies from each league that I could teach other players, and it helped me as a defensive back and coach.

As a football player, thankfully my years in Arizona were awesome. My first year was a great year. I set a lot of records. Even though we didn't win a lot of games, I think I was one of the bright spots on the team. I wasn't making great money, but still, I was a football player. I wasn't able to work in another career while playing, and so, like many have experienced, I was pigeonholed into being an athlete and not having any other sense of identity, which probably held me back after my football days ended.

I re-signed for a second year in Arizona with a really nice contract. We had a new up-and-coming coach with a lot to prove, a very smart guy and a very good coach. He had done a great job as an arena football coach, and he was as cutthroat as they come. I felt like because I was kind of an "inherited" player in the team for the new coach, I didn't fit into their group of favored ones.

I proved to this coach that I was a leader for his team, but early in the season I pulled my hamstring muscle completely. The coach treated me as if it was my fault that I had been hurt. I was singled-out for a lot of petty things, just because my injury. In one situation, for example, our team lived in apartments payed for by the team for players not from the city. We did everything together, so when half the football team was grilling, hanging out drinking, and doing other stuff one night at my apartment, I pretty much had to take the fall for everybody as I was strangely the only player called in about the incident. That's another point for you, athletes. Once you're in bad standing with coaches or an organization, don't give them a reason to release you or blame you for anything. If you value your craft and your job, do whatever it takes to make sure they understand you're going to handle your end of business and not take setbacks lightly.

I didn't take a stand, so I was always an easy target. Although there were ten or twelve other guys in the building with me, I took the heat for a lot of stuff that was going on, and for the first time ever I was cut from a football team. It was my second year in Arizona with one game left in the season. I had been out of playing in the games since week six with the hamstring injury, so it isn't like I could be blamed for losing, but I was released. I guess I was prideful but I really felt bad knowing that a coach I put my body on the line for would release me while I was injured. In spite of all I had been through to that point, it was a newly humbling experience being released for the first time in my career.

With the injury and release, I didn't know if I even wanted to continue to play football. But I made a decision. I decided to take all of it as motivation to say "Yes, I do want to continue." I rehabbed, worked out hard, and eventually signed on with another Canadian football team in Winnipeg, Manitoba: the Winnipeg Blue Bombers. It was the beginning of my next journey as a football player.

On my way to Winnipeg, I thought about the great ball clubs I'd had the honor to be a part of. One of the best parts of each was the fans. In addition to Nebraska's amazing red-blooded Husker fans and the New Orleans Saints' fantastic high-energy fans, I was blessed to be able to play for dedicated Edmonton Eskimos fans with a long, wild history of supporting their team. Arizona Rattlers fans were remarkable, too—some of the most loyal and kindhearted people I've met. In arena football, you only get twenty-four to thirty guys on the team roster so fans develop a very close and more personal bond with the team. I thank God that, no matter where I have been playing football, I have played for organizations with great supporters who love and follow their teams.

Chapter 7

Can't Stay Away (Back To Canada)

Being in Winnipeg, Manitoba, was a unique experience for me. After being through the highs and lows of life, as well as the highs and lows as a football player, I actually felt I was becoming more mature.

During training camp my first year in Winnipeg, a fellow teammate called me old school as we were warming up before a practice. "Old school" is basically the old man on the team, and up until that point I had always been one of the young ones on a roster. Just like that, I went from being a young buck to being old school; there was no in-between.

Don't get me wrong, I was still very competitive, still good at what I did. It was just a harsh realization that these younger guys who were fresh out of college were very motivated, hungry, and full of youth. It reminded me of the movie *Any Given Sunday* with Jamie Foxx, who played Willie Beaman, the up and coming young talented backup. The character, Willie Beamon, went in for Cap, who was the older quarterback played by Dennis Quaid. My situation was starting to feel like the same scenario, and I couldn't help but laugh to myself, even though it was my livelihood at stake. I learned to laugh at myself through difficult situations because I've learned that with time this negative experience will pass. If it's not going to kill you, it's only going to make you stronger and smarter. Their calling me old school just pushed me to be better.

KEYUO CRAVER SR.

It was obvious I was a veteran at this stage in my career, and I would do things like wait until training camp to get into shape as opposed to staying in shape the whole off-season. I knew my body and knew what it would take to get it to where I needed to be. At least, I *thought* I knew. That arrogance started to catch up with me... again.

I had a good first year in Winnipeg, but I wasn't a very loud, outgoing, flamboyant type of guy. And as a result of that, I didn't get a lot of attention or notoriety from the media or even the fans. I was however one of the guys in the locker room who a lot of the players respected and loved to talk to. I always kept people laughing. I was straight up and honest with people, as well. It seemed like I didn't have a lot of respect from the league, but in the locker room I was esteemed. That was most important to me then, being respected by my peers—the players I shared the field with. As long as I had their respect that was sufficient for me.

In fact, I was pretty laid back at this stage in my career and focused on really taking in my last years as a professional athlete. I didn't party that much and kept a low profile, but trouble somehow found me anyway. One night in Winnipeg, I dropped my roommate off at a club and used his car for the night while he was out with a few friends partying. I decided to stay in with a few teammates and play cards, and he eventually called me to come pick him up when he was done.

I was outside the club waiting for him to get to the car, but he didn't come out right away. As I waited in the car talking with a friend on the phone, I noticed a man walking towards my friend's car. The man knocked on my window. I thought he was drunk and just playing around, but he started kicking the car door and demanding that I get out of the car. He was under the impression I was driving *his* car. I knew he was out of his mind, but he was doing major damage to my friend's ride.

I told him that if he did not stop damaging my boy's ride, I'd have no choice but to get out of the car. He kicked with more authority. I decided to get out of the car, and when I did, he squared up with me, ready for a fight. I was thinking, *"Am I really about to fight this man over nothing—me, over thirty years old?"* As he rushed me, I sidestepped him and gave him a quick one-two to stop him from rushing at me. He stepped back and tried again, but I dodged him and gave him another quick two jabs, and then he fell to the ground.

I moved toward him, but he was flailing and moving around, so I decided to let him get up, because I was much quicker and more coordinated than him. I had on a white T-shirt and sweats. When I stepped back, I saw that my T-shirt was red all the way through. I couldn't believe it. This guy had pulled out a knife and was swinging it at me while he was on the ground. I felt around to see where I was hit, because I could not feel any pain anywhere. I found where most of the blood was coming from, and suddenly felt spooked: my life was in danger.

I went into ninja mode and game-planned my attack with this man. I would step in and get two, three hits and then back out and wait for him to make his next move. The intensity felt as if I was playing in a football game and my life was on the line. I was eventually able to knock him out. I used my fist and legs during this fight. Once he was on the ground, knocked out, two girls came out and screamed, "Please stop!" They knew the guy, but didn't have any idea how this had gotten started. I told them he had assaulted my friend's car, then me. I told them he pulled out a knife and stabbed me. They picked him up and took him to a car that was the exact same model as my friend's, except for the rims.

I made it back to my roommate's car and waited for him to come out. When he came to the car, he asked, "What the hell happened to you?" I told him the story, and he could not believe it. Not until I got home did I realize how lucky I had been. I had small stab wounds all over me, and his knife had sliced me on my arm very close to a vein. I didn't get stitches that night but just cleaned and bandaged it. When I went to practice the next day, I knew I had some explaining to do. I made up a horrible lie and told our trainer I had been moving a box of knives down the stairs and fell. He gave me the craziest look as if he knew I was full of it, but I left it at that. I look back at that incident and thank God for allowing me to still be here, because it could have easily gone wrong in so many ways.

In football, we had a decent year, but we had a coach who was kind of a hothead. He was a good coach and a great guy, but the organization got rid of him after his first year. Then, in my second year, they brought in a guy with the complete opposite personality of the previous coach. He was an up-and-coming young coach, and he was trying to prove himself in the CFL. I didn't believe his agenda or the way he went about business was fitting for what it takes to build a championship team. He was one of those coaches who comes across as judgmental. I noticed right away that he only took the time to get to know certain players, usually the highest paid or most popular players. In my opinion, he was a little arrogant and didn't really get to know all of his players. As a result, a lot of players didn't trust him, and I was one of them. I definitely got that vibe from him that he didn't want me on the team. I was going into my tenth year of professional football, at thirty years old, so maybe there wasn't much he felt he would be able to tell me or teach me. No matter how nice I tried to come across, I felt like he had his mind made up that he didn't want me there.

In one particular instance during a preseason game, he sat out a few guys who were younger, inexperienced players, basically assuring them that they had made the team. However, he had me travel with players who were still fighting to make the team. I'm used to adversity, and used to drama, and I guess he didn't know who he was dealing with. At least this is what I told myself. In this particular game I played well, and made it hard for him to release me. Because of my performance in that game, he couldn't justify cutting me, and I ended up making the team. It sure felt like God's way of looking out for me and letting me know that He had my back. One of the assistant coaches confirmed my suspicions and told me on our plane ride home after the game that it was indeed true that the head coach was looking for a reason to release me, but my performance in the game assured that it would not happen now. Even if the head coach was really trying to put me in a position to fail, when God is on your side, you won't fail. No matter how bad it looks, you can overcome it with patience and trust, and don't forget hard work: put feet to that faith.

Then came week one of our football season. The beginning of the CFL season starts around Canada's Independence Day so there is great excitement and gorgeous weather to kick off the season. As we prepared for our first game, I thought about what really mattered to me. I might have a coach who didn't respect me, but I had so much love and respect in the locker room from young guys whom I was able to mentor. Years later many of them did great things in their career and it's been great to know I saw the potential in them years before.

So, picture it, the referee blows the whistle and we have kickoff underway to start the game, and you know what happened in the first quarter of my last year of professional football? I tore my ACL. How funny is that? Here was this coach who wanted any reason to release me and get me off his team but now due to injury that wasn't going to be possible because the team cannot release an injured player.

I wasn't even mad. I laughed about it, because I knew the head coach was waiting for an opportunity to release me, which most people would look at as a negative thing, but I saw it as a blessing. Due to my injury, the coach had to see me out to the very end of the season. I got to rehab on their dollar and to look this man in the eye every day just to let him know I knew he didn't want me there. I was still there and wasn't going anywhere.

Irony is a kick in the teeth, and there was so much irony in that situation that I couldn't help but thank God for bringing me through it, for allowing me to use that negative situation and for turning it into positive opportunities. I could see the same dynamics with a lot of my circumstances after my career at Nebraska. It truly has made me a smarter man, a more humble man, and a more honest man. I will never turn my back on the failures I've had in life, because they have made me who I am today. My failures have just as much if not more to do with the person I am and will become as my successes do.

There was another benefit to my injury. The track star Canadian female I fell in love with in Edmonton, and I had our beloved son Issa that previous year also. I got to spend a whole year rehabbing for two or three hours per day, and then spending the rest of the day loving and spending time with him. His mother and I lived in Osborne Village which is a very artistic and hip part of Winnipeg, lined with great restaurants. It also had a ton of history, culture, and boasts a ratio of six or seven females to every male, so there were always beautiful women around.

KEYUO CRAVER SR.

My son's mother was a Canadian, and we made a commitment to be together. No matter what, we were going to stick it out, but when my football career was over, we ran into a problem. I didn't know what I wanted to do as far as work. One thing I did know was that I would have to go back to the States by law. When that time came, she didn't want any part of starting over in life there without income or a concrete plan. That was difficult, because I really thought I was in love. I thought I was finally with somebody I was ready to spend the rest of my life with.

As in all things, if it's not meant to happen, it just won't happen. So, I finished up my contract, rehabbed up to almost a full physical recovery, and with my visa almost about to expire, it was time to go back to the U.S.

I was coming off a major injury, without a lot of cash to my name, and moving back to the States to figure out what life had in store for me after football. I had many friends in the U.S, some very close who I felt would have my back. But when word got out that I was moving back without a lot to offer, none of those "friends" opened their door for me nor reached out to help while I tried to get things figured out.

Then, one of my big brothers in the Husker community who I was friends with, but had not necessarily been that close to previously, kindly offered to have me move into his home rent-free until I got some plans put together. To this day, our friendship has grown into a close brotherhood. My point is that you never know who God will place into your life to be an angel on earth. I would never have guessed it would be this person, but I also never guessed that people who had called me brother would watch me struggle, knowing their help could make a difference. Once again, instead of viewing this as an obstacle, I viewed it as an opportunity. It didn't do anything but motivate me to get my life together, and that is exactly what I did. I never asked for any handouts. Just as in sports, I worked my way up from the bottom to get to the top.

I thank the Lord for the adversity I endured as well as the truths that were discovered through the challenges I faced. I've decided I won't be fake in anyone's life. If I can help a close friend, I will, but if it's not possible I have no problem expressing that to him or her. It's important to be honest. I didn't picture my journey going this way, but I'm thankful for the experiences. It has taught me so much about myself and about the many different kinds of people who come into your life. There are true friends, and there are temporary people who come just to teach you a valuable lesson. I am grateful for each and every person and encounter.

Chapter 8

I Never Saw That Coming

Because it had such a powerful effect on my life, and because it has such a destructive effect in the lives of so many others, I want to talk about my history of drug use. I believe, if those who are struggling with addiction can see the progression of it in my life, it could help them identify it in their own lives—and do something about it.

The first time I smoked weed was my senior year of high school. I threw up and didn't touch it again until after a couple of years in college. I really did not see that as an issue because I didn't do it routinely. It was one of those things that I did when the opportunity presented itself, not an everyday thing.

My first-time drinking was in high school, during graduation. I got drunk and had a car wreck, and I made up a story about hitting a deer and lied to my grandmother. That was the first time I drank alcohol. I started to drink a lot in college, mostly on the weekends, at parties. It was what people did over the weekend, never really thinking about the consequences.

In 2002, I got a DUI in Scottsdale, AZ. I was extremely immature, naive, and not nearly as focused or as prepared as one should be in preparing to go to the NFL. I did not really understand the position I was in and the amount of attention you get when you're a young black male with opportunities to make money. The night of my DUI, I learned I was a target. The cops pulled up behind me before I was able to put my vehicle in reverse.

After I was drafted into the NFL, as a consequence of the DUI, I entered a drug treatment program required by the NFL. That was when I basically started to learn about addiction and treatment. Honestly, now that I look back, it was a blessing. My first year in the NFL, I had no issues. I played very well. I got praises from my coaches.

A little after halfway through the first season, I suffered a knee injury, which turned my experience upside down. I went from being one of the players who was praised, talked about and talked to, to someone who was ignored and I didn't really feel needed. Arrogance, self-pity, depression and complacency set in, and I coped by going out and drinking. I got validation from others in the clubs, only because I played in the NFL. Most people told me what I wanted to hear and not what I really needed to hear.

I rarely used marijuana while I played in the NFL, but I did smoke occasionally. I had fun and partied, but I drank more than I smoked. Pot had a negative effect on me. I withdrew, and I really did not want to be around people. I failed four drug tests over my three years at New Orleans. I was suspended for an entire year. The NFL did everything they could to educate me, give me treatment, and help me. When you are young and think you know everything and you haven't really experienced rock bottom, all that knowledge doesn't really resonate with you. My arrogance led to my eventual demise. I self-indulged, didn't work for a year, because the NFL had suspended me and I didn't know what would happen next.

* * *

Initially I felt like the organization I was working for really didn't have my back at the time, and I believed that was why I had to learn the hard way. Without a doubt, I feel a bit differently about that now. The NFL offers valuable and potentially life-changing accommodations to their athletes. Unfortunately, young athletes, including myself at the time, often don't realize it until it's too late. The league assigns people specifically to help with these kinds of challenges, but athletes usually meet these available resources when they are facing a pressured situation that is often a result of something negative. It's very easy to become defensive and even more withdrawn when one has to open up about issues that may be going on.

I believe, if the league, along with former players and current players, would develop a more proactive approach to informing new players about the struggles and pitfalls they will potentially encounter over the years, it could be very beneficial for all parties involved. That said, it's not all up to the league officials and staff. I encourage current NFL athletes to talk to veteran players on the team, or player personnel, to get more information about ways that one can get support and help.

In addition to getting help with bad situations such as drugs, alcohol and other destructive behaviors, it's a great idea to get an early start considering your career after football. I wasn't smart enough to do it, but most of us will never have these types of support available to us again, so why not use them to the fullest potential? Most players will not be lucky enough to make a long-lasting career of being an NFL athlete, so it makes sense to maximize the opportunity while you can.

The NFL has done a great job of making resources available for former players, too. One useful program the NFL has awarded former players with is called the Trust Fund. Former players who meet certain requirements can apply for, join, and receive services through the Trust, getting help for a wide variety of situations—from starting a business, to finding financial aid for college, and even handling medical emergencies.

I believe the NFL is definitely taking the necessary steps to make the sport safer and make the hazards more transparent for players and fans. It's obvious that the league cares about the well-being of their players and the integrity of the sport.

* * *

Drugs and alcohol. Does it happen one step at a time until you suddenly notice it has taken over your life? Or does it take you down like a strike of lightning? For me, it came crashing down all of a sudden, or so it appeared at the time. There were several factors way beforehand that definitely were warning signs of worse things to come, but I chose not to listen to them.

At first, the drinking and partying did not seem to affect me, but as I spent more time doing it over the course of the season, my body began to wear down. Mentally, you try to tell yourself this is not the case, but performance doesn't lie. The role that substances play in damaging your body is so silent, but it eventually takes a major toll on you physically and mentally. I learned the hard way.

If you are fortunate enough to have the opportunity to play professional football, please consider the short amount of time you will be able to play at that level. Don't do anything to sabotage yourself. I encourage you to love and enjoy life as everyone should, but don't take for granted the blessing set before you by selfishly making choices that destroy those blessings. I know, for me personally, I would have been able to accomplish a lot more had I at least taken some control over the time I spent partying and having fun. I got caught up in praising my gift and not my Giver of the gift. I wanted all the credit for something borrowed. I learned the hard way and I hope my story helps people to avoid some of the same pitfalls.

Many have wondered if I did hard drugs while I was a professional athlete. So many people *assumed* I did due to the negative stereotypes of athletes portrayed by the media and TV shows. The truth of the matter is, although I can't deny I took advantage of partying, drinking, and smoking weed, I was still aware enough to know I didn't want to find out if my addiction would apply to harder substances out there. I was terrified of that, because I knew what potentially could happen, even as low as I was at that point in my life. I was still looked at and treated as if I was addicted to hard substances, such as crack or meth. In all honesty, it could just as well have been hard drugs in some ways, because the results were the same: I still lost a lot of what I worked for.

I believe everything happens for a reason, and if there is any chance for some of you to learn from my experiences and not have to go down the same road of destruction that I went down, it's worth laying this all out on the line for you. And please don't forget, you don't have to be a football player to learn from the things that happened to me.

What can I say to help athletes and other young people to overcome the temptation of drugs and alcohol? Obviously not trying drugs or alcohol would be what I suggest first, but I know it's not realistic for so many. For many it's too late to avoid drugs and alcohol altogether. They are already a part of many people's lives. For those who are faced with battling these demons, the first thing you need to know is that you are not alone! Help is closer than you think and available for you at any time.

I encourage anyone who is struggling with drugs or alcohol use to first find a way to want to make a change for yourself. There is no way anyone can help you if you truly don't make up your mind to help yourself. Find someone you respect and trust to talk to about what you are dealing with. Then find out what resources are available to you—at school, in your community, from trusted adults and leaders. People who genuinely care about you will do whatever is necessary to make sure you are safe and using every resource that can benefit you.

Addiction or substance misuse is difficult for the person directly involved, but it also horribly affects that person's family, spouse, and close friends as well. My family and I went through a lot together when I got suspended from the NFL for a year, and we are now very open with each other about our everyday lives and health.

I encourage the families and close friends of those directly affected by drugs or alcohol to not be afraid to speak up if you are noticing self-destructive behavior. It's very subtle and easy to overlook at first, but when you do start to notice the difference in behaviors of your loved one, please let them know what you are seeing. It could be the difference between life and death for the person you love. Whether that individual wants to hear you or not, a true friend will keep their close one's best interests at heart and say what needs to be said. If the person chooses not to listen, tell a spouse or relative close to them what is going on, and figure out a plan or intervention together.

Family can sometimes mean all the difference in the world to a person with a drug or alcohol problem. I know this because of my own kids. I would overcome anything to be able to be a better dad to them. My children are my greatest motivators, as I mentioned with having Keyuo Jr. in 2005, which helped me while I was dealing with some very difficult problems. If you remember, it was right around the time when I was dealing with being suspended from the NFL. During that awful time for me, his birth gave me something meaningful to focus on: his happiness. It made me focus less on my depressing situation. Being able to simply hold my son and have him with me every day helped me believe in myself. Find your motivation. Sometimes it's as close as your own family members.

* * *

During the height of my partying phase, even though I felt as if I was alone, I truly wasn't. Not only were my family and good friends there if only I had reached out, but the NFL did everything possible to get me anything I could have possibly needed to help me with my self-destructive behaviors and substance misuse issues. After my first year, having failed a couple of drug tests, I took outpatient treatment in downtown New Orleans. Can you imagine how hard that was? I was a twenty-something year-old who had never really had to deal with these types of consequences.

Looking back, I know I didn't take it as seriously as my problem really was. How can you expect a kid to not be tempted when he has to drive through the French Quarter every day to get to work? It was just too easy to stop at a nice restaurant and get a daiquiri at any downtown corner. That was no excuse to not take my career and livelihood for granted. I have always known that I could overcome obstacles, so even if I did think it might become a problem, I got complacent and it caught up with me. Unfortunately, I still wasn't done learning those lessons after my first year in the NFL.

I remember the wide variety of people in that outpatient program. It was strange, because everyone was so different and was there for different reasons. The information the program provided us was interesting to me and very helpful. We learned all about addiction, including recognizing why it happens and what triggers a person to go deep into that behavior. I started to realize it is very hard to change that behavior without understanding the harm that a person is doing to themselves with the drugs and alcohol. Obviously, this program didn't fix my issues right away, but it did equip me with more knowledge about addiction—and myself.

At that time, I don't think I was quite mature enough to understand how blessed I had been in life up until that point, or that this could turn into a major life-shaking problem for me. The thing that stuck with me most from outpatient treatment was seeing that substance abuse affects people differently. For some people, addiction is obvious, but I was still able to function. In fact, I thought it looked like nothing was wrong on the outside, but those who really knew me said they saw me as more withdrawn and shorter in conversations. Outpatient treatment allowed me to look into the mirror at myself and do less blaming of people around me. The NFL checked on me on a regular basis my entire career, but not until it was too late did I completely understand that my own selfishness wouldn't allow me to humble myself to receive help from one of the strongest enterprises in the world.

Since I didn't learn my lesson after being sent to outpatient treatment during my second year in the NFL, I eventually failed another drug test and was asked to go to inpatient treatment at a famous center in Boston, Massachusetts. With this suspension, I was taken out of four games without pay. When I first arrived in Boston, it was late at night and the place was surrounded by trees and woods. It was during the Halloween season, and I remember it was a creepy feeling being there, in a brand-new city and environment.

When I awoke the next morning, with the daylight I could see this place was beautiful and peaceful. It was perfect for its purpose. I met the clinicians and got a rundown on how things would be the few weeks that would follow. It was overwhelming and intimidating. The first week was probably the most difficult, because the routine was so new to me. There were other people in the group-home-like setting, but again we were all there for different reasons. This center was huge, and offered extensive services, from inpatient treatment to come-and-go-as-you-please outpatient options. Our schedule included meetings all day on campus, and all meals were eaten together. I was the only professional athlete, but none of that matters at a place like that.

The media portrays addiction as a problem of lower-income neighborhoods, but in Boston I quickly learned this is not the case. There were doctors, professors, politicians and nurses who struggled with addiction and participated in the groups that I was a part of. It was fascinating to see the denial of certain behaviors by some of the smartest and most successful people I have been around. Seeing them try to outsmart their addictions and demons made it easier for me realize I had done the same thing in my own life. My consequences proved I had not been making the right decisions, no matter how smart I was.

These were some of the most difficult weeks of my life, because I did not get to see my family or even talk to them much, but a lot of good came out of it. I finally was able to see that I did have a problem with drinking and partying, and a strong affection for smoking weed, too. Perhaps most importantly, it became clear that if I wanted to see changes in my life, even with all the treatment I was getting from some of the best doctors and clinicians in the world, I still had to make the decision to want to change.

I wish I could say they did, but my struggles did not stop with treatment. However, I picked up some very valuable information that has helped me to this day. I still have work to do on myself and demons I face every day, but I am no longer in denial about my shortcomings. One very important aspect of dealing with addiction that these experiences taught me was that self-reflection and meditation (just like Mrs. White taught me) are very important in getting yourself to peace and knowing yourself better—and keeping yourself in a better state of mind. Another important principle of treatment that has helped me the most since my inpatient and outpatient treatment experiences is purposefully reaching out to my close family and friends that I know love me and have my best interests at heart. I have given them the green light to be honest with me about my behaviors, and I have asked them to please call me out if they notice me changing or becoming destructive.

Chapter 9

CONTROL

Control is a strange thing. Those who crave it are usually those who have the least control. We'd much rather stay in control of a situation than find out we're wrong; it's easier to handle emotionally. But life is humbling. I had a major event take place in my life for me to finally be aware of my negative desire for control. You may go almost your entire life before something happens to allow you to see things differently.

I became more arrogant and controlling as I became more successful. Professional athletes are looked up to, and oftentimes that attention makes one feel invincible or entitled. Rather than find a way to use this control to do something positive, I used it to feed my already-growing ego. Wanting that type of control really showed how much I lacked mentally and emotionally as a man. I needed other people to believe I was in control of my surroundings, and that hindered me from allowing myself to grow and learn more about myself as a person.

The primary example of my control issues would be the relationships I've had with women. Since I was a young kid, I have been obsessed with wanting the perfect woman. I can't put the blame on anyone. Truthfully, we always get what we ask for, but it's not always a good thing. For me seeing a beautiful woman is very gratifying. For men in general, this is usually the case. However, since I've been an athlete most of my life, I've had an advantage over some men: I have always been around women who wanted to know me, and I liked it. I would use the fact that I was a prominent athlete to get (or try to get) a woman I thought was attractive. It was "mutual usury" I guess you could say. Maybe they were using *me* because I was an athlete, but I was using *them* because they were beautiful.

To be real, it's not hard to get women when you have a lot of money or are a professional athlete. People love athletes, and it's easy to see why. Athletes, especially those in the college and professional ranks, are very confident and charming. In my experience, most women get the impression that confidence and talent transfer into all other aspects of the athlete's life, but this assumption is so far from the truth, I almost find it sad. With confidence, talent, and charm at a person's disposal, arrogance often tags along. Without a shadow of a doubt, I displayed these characteristics, both good and bad. But I'm not trying to justify the bad side. There is no excuse for total and complete arrogance.

My arrogance when it came to women did catch up with me, but it took me a long time to learn my lesson. Starting in my freshman year of college, I was destined to learn the hard way. I thought I was pretty smart. I don't think I came off like a "know it all," but I sure liked to pretend I knew all. I assumed I was smart enough to talk to two women at the same time. Sounds pretty normal? No, I am ashamed to admit that I had to step it up a notch and try to talk to two women that stayed on the same dorm floor as me. I lived in Abel Hall, legendary on UNL's campus for freshman notoriously having too much fun and being loud.

At the time, there was a very popular song by Brandy and Monica, two famous R&B singers of the day, called "The Boy Is Mine." In the music video for the song, the "boy" in the video tries to manage dating both women at the same time, but eventually they find out about each other and turn the tables on him by setting him up. At the end of the video one of the women calls and plans to come over to his apartment. When she arrives, she knocks on his door. He checks the peep hole to see that it is her, and opens the door smiling with his arms wide open. His girlfriend is there smiling as well, but as the door creeps open wider he notices his other woman standing there also. Those smiles quickly turn upside down and the women rip into the man, and rightfully so.

KEYUO CRAVER SR.

Much to my surprise and horror, one night as my roommate Demo and I were watching BET network's "The Basement" in our room, this same scene played itself out. There was a knock at the door and I opened it to see one of my sweeties, and I reached out to greet her with a hug... and as the door opened wider, I saw my other lady friend that I was talking to standing there with her arms folded and eyes cocked like a pistol. BUSTED! The two of them stormed my dorm room, and my roommate ran a record 40-yard dash out and down the hall. I couldn't do anything but let the two of them yell at me and push on me. Nothing like this had ever happened to me so I sat there like a little kid, feeling embarrassed and ashamed. I apologized to both women, but I seriously felt pretty dumb. I was so freaked out that I went overboard: that same night I rededicated my life to Christ, had Bible study, and prayed trying to prove to myself that I was not a bad person. I actually ran into one of the women involved in this story at a tailgate a couple of years ago, and we laughed so hard about our crazy experience at Abel Hall.

Unfortunately, this incident and many others I had as a young man were not enough to get my attention or teach me a lesson. It was just the beginning of my arrogance and hunger for control.

Once I started thinking about settling down, I wanted control over the type of woman I settled down with—the way she looked and the way she acted. That desire for control led me to much of the stress and pain I went through and made it hard for these women to leave, because I am very convincing. On the flip side, it also made it easy for them to leave as soon as things didn't go according to plan.

I love all my beautiful children, and I have no regrets in that regard. What would my life be like without them? They are the best thing that has EVER happened to me. But the fact that I only wanted to be with their mothers for selfish reasons brought me, them, and their mothers a lot of pain. At a certain point in my life I did finally have a clear realization of this, and it left me exposed, without excuse, and no one to blame but myself.

Add to that the regret I have felt about having put the different women whom I cared for in the position of having to leave...

Add to that the fact that I can't be with my children every day…

It's not a pretty picture. I am just grateful that I've come to the other side of the need for control. They were expensive lessons, but I learned them.

* * *

I would argue that most athletes struggle more with navigating everyday life than they struggle with the pressure of being an athlete. When you represent people's favorite teams, many people put high expectations on every aspect of your life, and that pressure has the power to dull the joy of reaching your dream. This is truly devastating when you realize it. When you graduate from college, you are still very young and not very experienced in handling life's pressures. Then, when you become a pro, you're making more money than almost everyone you know. Things can get very complicated.

I had grown up loving football, playing football, and watching football— and when I began to play, I was very good at it. As I got older, I began to really feel the pressures of people's expectations of me, piling onto my own expectations of myself. It seemed, within the blink of an eye, others who saw my potential tried to capitalize on it. I became arrogant and bold in my appetite for life— always looking for ways to make myself look good. Then, on the way to the pros, before I knew it, I had multiple kids by different women, debt before I even began to make money, and so many fake smiles and handshakes that I had no clue who was being true to me. It fed my desire to control even more.

Not only was I addicted to control, I had a tendency to try to control things in my life that were *out of my control*. I still work on that to this very day. When you encounter a lot of success, not many people challenge or question your decisions or actions. This distorts your perception, and you tend to lose sight of reality. People will feed you attention just to get what they want from you. This gave me a false sense of control. Although it felt like I was in control, I wasn't. Not even close.

Worrying so much about dominating others led to losing control of myself. Again, the signs were there in college. When I first got to Nebraska the summer before my freshman year, I was a little out of control. It felt so good to have some independence. Don't get me wrong, I loved growing up in Harleton, which was a reasonably sheltered place, but college was the first time I had ever really been on my own. I wasn't even 18, but I tried to act as if I was more mature and knew how to handle things on my own... especially when it came to fitting in at parties with my teammates.

This false sense of control affected my daily life for years, and I didn't realize how lost I was until it was too late. It's important to understand, to even become an elite athlete, you have to learn to be good at executing small details, every day, diligently—going to the weight room, working out when you don't feel like it, going the extra mile consistently—because you *want to*. This is the "good" type of control. In high school, I didn't need validation from the media or fans. Heck, no one even knew about me. I lived in the small details, like I just described above. But when I got a taste of success in college, earned All-American honors and the accolades started swirling, I got used to the validation from the outside, I stopped working on those details. As an athlete, you do need control, self-conrol, for your craft. Had I been humble enough to continue to do the small things I had done to get to the pros, I know I would have been better equipped to handle some of the stressors and situations in a more positive way.

As an NFL player, the reality is that the people that come into your life often just like to be around you because of your status. Their excitement towards you really feeds the ego, and you want to keep it like this, feeling good! This definitely describes my life at the time, and it was how I wanted it, so I controlled who I allowed to be in my life. What I perceived as control was actually just an exchange: I got attention and they got to be close to someone who was "famous," or whatever it was they were looking for. Once I was no longer associated with the NFL, the illusion disappeared and all those fake people were suddenly gone too, and I couldn't do anything about it. The exchange crumbled, and suddenly it became crystal clear how unhealthy and toxic it was. I wasn't in control of anything. By the time I realized it, nothing was left and no one was there anymore. This opened my eyes to who did genuinely care about me, because they stuck with me when I had nothing to offer but me.

I PEED & FORGOT

* * *

Actually, the ability to control can be a great gift if used positively, but it comes with the responsibility to use this skill and each situation in a healthy way. If used properly and effectively by someone in a position of leadership, control can lead to more opportunity and side benefits that bring positive results for everyone involved. If you're in a position of influence like I was, please be mindful of this lesson.

I used my control selfishly. I learned the hard way that when you try to control another fully capable human being, you are setting yourself up for failure. Not only is that person different from you mentally, but he or she also has a completely different perspective based on their own experiences. You usually don't realize how ineffective being controlling is until you have pushed that person too far away. It's also hard to gain back the trust that was once there. Once a relationship has reached that stage, you feel the loss and it can come down hard on you in the form of depression, self-hatred, or other damaging emotions.

If any of these things are sounding familiar to you, don't let your control issues drive you to depression or even worse, self-harm. Ask for help if you need to. It may sound simple, or maybe impossible, but try to do better. Own your mistakes and learn from them. Understand it's healthier and a lot safer to only worry about what you can control in *your own* life.

When a person struggles to let go of unhealthy control tendencies, it's not easy to make a change. But it can be done. The first thing to do is recognize the problem and *admit* you may have these types of issues. This first step is often the hardest challenge. Many of us don't even know we have control issues, so there's no way to address them. You can start by truly getting a sense of yourself. Knowing your limits, your strengths, and your weaknesses plays a major role in learning how to get in control of yourself, which ironically helps you let go of the need to control everything else around you.

There are some lessons we just have to go through in life, but the lack of self-control can lead to long-lasting, regrettable behavior and it's not worth the risk if you can help it. You can't undo what's been done, so be aware that once you commit to something, the consequences are with you forever. Really grasping this fact can work in your favor. Remind yourself what you've lost, and use your regret to help keep you from repeating your mistakes.

Open your eyes and try to identify certain situations or events that give you a clue, let your conscience talk, and actually listen. At the height of my partying days in New Orleans, I became pretty inactive. Rather than train or work on my craft, I chilled at home during the day and partied all night. It was a clue that I didn't heed. I was out of shape and out of control, but I would never admit it. Then again, as my grandmother used to tell me, "The truth don't lie."

Another time, I was visiting home during the off-season after my second year in the NFL. I was catching up with my dad and one of my close friends about life and things going on in Harleton. A friend I had known for more than 20 years started talking about football and how he should've gone to college like me, teasing me by saying he knew he was just as fast as me and he figured he could beat me running. I was in no shape to be racing anyone, which was sad considering my profession, but my pride allowed me to ignore my own sad condition. We went outside and lined up. I won, but it was too close for comfort. I knew it was actually a loss for me, and was an unexpected wake up call. It was a small step towards me seeing how partying and not staying focused could bring me down quickly.

It's important to understand that this is a life-long process, so please be patient. Don't get discouraged and react negatively when changes in your life don't reward you right away. Keep your eye on the goal: an honest life with people who love you for who you are, not because you control them, but because they respect you and want to be with you. This can happen when you are truly honest with yourself and those close to you.

Another pitfall to be aware of is feeling the need to do exactly as other successful people that you admire. Although one should definitely watch and learn from those types of people, you should be mindful that everyone is different. Don't expect their outcome to be yours. For example, if you're not a vocal person, don't put pressure on yourself because someone else is good at it. This is a mistake. Rather, focus on your own strengths and find ways to exercise your own unique qualities so you can help yourself and your team in ways that only you can. Stay focused on the strength within yourself as a person and athlete.

In the end, I realized that being controlling didn't get me anywhere. It only led to a lot of anger and resentment of people—me towards them and them towards me—but it was absolutely no one's fault except mine. Being conscious of this reality made me regret a lot of choices I made and behavior I exhibited. It made life rather embarrassing, because it revealed how much control I actually *didn't* have. It affected relationships with my family and close friends, because I was a lot less humble, a quality that I value in myself now.

Growing more humble has allowed me to be more open to listening to others, which has produced positive fruit in so many ways, and not just as an athlete. It also has allowed me to enjoy life more and not take myself so seriously. Now, with humility on my side, I don't need validation from others to know my worth. That kind of thing—validation from others—feels good to hear, but I know my purpose and my heart now, and that's what I try to focus on instead.

This new perspective has also been very beneficial for me in terms of work and school. Having more humility and understanding has truly made me better in every aspect of my life. Before, I worked so hard to control each circumstance trying to achieve these things, but now it was starting to come effortlessly. I still have so much more improvement to go, but I've come a long way. Being controlling took so much away from me. It diverted me from doing more positive things. Perhaps most fundamentally, this behavior stopped me from being able to grow as a person mentally and spiritually. I was so self-consumed that I didn't get to know myself on a personal level. I'm thankful that I can see it now, but I'm warning you, having your eyes opened to these truths is hard for anyone to see this about themselves. But it's worth it.

If I could only get one thing across to you, the reader of this book, to help you overcome controlling behaviors, it would be this: remember your upbringing. Even if it wasn't perfect, never forgetting where you came from is so very important. It can keep you focused and put things in perspective when you find yourself lost. For athletes, this is really important to keep you grounded. You have people who love you, people who tried hard to teach you what they know and want the best for you. Listen to them. Remember the lessons of your childhood.

One last thing: People come and go, money comes and goes, possessions come and go, but please understand that your character and attitude will always follow you and be a part of who you are. Your character and attitude are two things you actually can have control over. Don't try to impose your control issues on other people. You will push them further away from you, and you will also lose yourself.

I thank God for humbling me early on and teaching me to deal with negativity, devils, and demons in my life. I use the terms "devils" and "demons" to refer to negative people and situations. No one can negotiate with the devil. I tried to, and my life reflected this truth because of the situations I found myself in over and over.

All my problems, addictions, setbacks, and failures in life are not completely solved or fixed. However, I am just more equipped and focused on the right things, which has helped me navigate out of some of my most difficult times. I love people but I needed to learn how to sit with myself and get to know myself on a more personal level. This is hard to say, so I'm sure it's even more difficult to understand, but I actually have gotten more control of things in my life since I was able to let go of my control issues. As I decrease my arrogance and let my spirit and mind focus on the right things, handling difficult situations has been much easier.

I think the hardest part of all this growth has been realizing that my previous choices, attitudes, and actions didn't really help the people in my life to grow. In fact, I know many times the results of our relationship were the opposite. In owning up to my stuff, I'm opening myself up to a lot of judgment. But I am inspired by what the apostle Paul wrote in the book of Romans: "*Let us stop judging one another. Instead, decide not to put anything in the way of a brother or sister. Don't put anything in their way that would make them trip and fall.*" (14:13, NIRV) I have *decided* that I don't want to be the cause of other's pain anymore, as far as that depends on me.

Chapter 10

What's Next?

I had to hit rock bottom in order to learn certain truths, and to grow, and I have. Although there was a still a chance that I could compete and play in the NFL after I was suspended for a year, I think God protected me from digging myself deeper into my demons. Moving to Canada was one of the most serene and reflective periods of my life. I learned a lot about myself because I had been through so much those previous couple of years. My experience in Canada helped me get to know myself better, and allowed me to really start taking life after football more serious.

Canada was also key for me because I played football for some great organizations and started realizing that the blessing of being a professional athlete was really short-lived and that I needed to start thinking about life after football. So that's what I did. Although I was talented enough to continue to compete and play at a higher level, my mind was on figuring out what I wanted to do with my life after football.

That's why I moved back to Lincoln, Nebraska after retiring from the CFL in 2011. I knew I loved helping people, working with people and helping them become better. I knew I could do it in that special city. When I graduated college in 2001, I figured that in a few years I would be retired and settled down after playing in the NFL. Boy was I wrong! Despite all the things I had done, it was hard grasping the reality of what my life had become. I am not bitter or angry, but this journey was nothing close to what I had imagined for myself. I could have easily found a million excuses to feel sorry for myself, but I refused to give up. No matter how many people gave up on me, I would never give up on myself, and with that attitude I was able to humble myself and begin my next journey with an open mind.

When I first moved back to Nebraska, the first job I got was for a gentleman who had a concrete pouring company. I coached his son on a Little League football team at the time. This gentleman was Hispanic, and although I appreciated the job, it was humbling—even embarrassing. On the football field, I had been known as a very hardworking and dedicated man, willing to go the extra mile, and I quickly learned that hardworking skill didn't translate into this new job. There were eight or nine other workers, all Hispanic, and there I was, the lone African American male.

The first day working with these professional concrete pourers, they did not take it easy on me. I had to keep up with them, and they did not slow down for me. I am not a quitter, so I really put my effort into it and tried very hard. They would look at me and say things in Spanish, and I knew they were talking about me. Rather than getting upset or bothered by it, I communicated nonverbally because my Spanish is terrible. I pointed to my arm and said "es no bueno, giving the thumb down signal, Para Tus es muy bueno, as I gave them the two thumbs up signal and pointed to all of them. They burst into laughter, and I couldn't help but to laugh hysterically as well even though I knew they were laughing at me and not with me. It was a funny moment, probably the only one from that experience, but I still learned something. It was clear to all of us that I was not ready for a career in pouring concrete. I sincerely thanked the gentleman for giving me an opportunity to make money, but that job was not for me.

After a couple more odd jobs, I got a job at a community center working with young kids. I knew I loved coaching and working with youth, so I looked for jobs that fit that description. Being able to help kids gave me a purpose and positive motivation. After a couple of odd-jobs I then found a job working with an organization that helps adults with developmental disabilities called RHD-Nebraska.

I love working with youth and adults with developmental disabilities. Whether it's coaching (which is definitely one of my passions), mentoring, or teaching, I love engaging minds that are eager to learn and to get better.

I PEED & FORGOT

Working in these fields posed challenges different from what I was used to, but I enjoyed it because I could see the positive impact that is made by helping people reach their goals. Both youth and adults with developmental disabilities are very honest and I admire that trait more than anything. The truth allows one to grow and become a better person. My success in this field really gave me validation that helping others is what drives me to be who I am, and it kept me humble.

Of all the fields I've worked in, coaching is a gift that I know God wants me to continue to learn and grow in. I almost feel the same intensity as a coach that I did as a player. The main difference I notice is the anxiety is a lot easier to deal with as a coach for me personally. The main reason I love coaching is not that my body will be safe from crushing contact, it's because some of the best lessons that I have learned in life have come from coaches that cared about me as a person and not just an athlete. Focusing on helping others become the best that they can be will only make them greater at their sport and everything else they do. To be able to teach kids about life lessons from my own experiences helps them understand that they are not alone!

It was not until I found a job working at a public school as a retention specialist, which is a fancy way of saying In-School Suspension Technician, spending time with high-school students who may need a place to decompress or process a certain situation or feeling that could potentially be negative, that I immediately knew this was a place that I wanted to be. For Nebraska, Lincoln High is very diverse, but what I loved most about the school was the atmosphere. This was the first job I had since retiring from playing professional football that felt just as rewarding and gratifying on the inside. Lincoln High is such a unique school and I learned a lot from the students, administrators, teachers, all the way up to the custodians that worked there. Being able to impact young minds positively and honestly is such an enormous blessing for me. Having this position and also being able to coach my 1st love filled a void that I had been missing for some time. I stopped working there to focus on this dream of mine, writing my book, but those three years working at The High were some of my best ever!

Knowing I still have to pay bills, I stayed with my other job and worked more hours. At RHD-Nebraska is an organization that provides residential support to individuals with intellectual disabilities. RHD specializes in providing true-person-centered services to help clients live a meaningful and successful life in their communities. I learn as much from the clients I work with as they do from me. Working there made me see how many small things I take for granted everyday.

Mental health is a prevalent topic in our society, and the more knowledgeable the public is about it, the better it will be for the community and the individuals being served. One of the most important goals for my clients is building positive relationships in the community.

What I admire most about my clients is the fact that they don't let their disabilities define them. This is especially important to me because it inspires me to stay positive and not let my negative setbacks define me. They aren't perfect, no one is, and it's very humbling and uplifting to watch them work hard in spite of the innumerable setbacks they experience everyday. Watching them stay resilient and not quit on themselves motivates me. Since I have worked for RHD I find it harder to feel sorry for myself. I have used my time working there to grow and learn more about me. I am able to find inspiration in the smallest gestures and I know working for RHD helped open my eyes more to see that.

I began thinking about what I had gone through in my life and how many challenges I had overcome, and I started wondering how I might be able to turn my bad experiences to good. I really loved both of my jobs, but with a drive to impact people on a larger scale, I decided that it was time I took a chance on myself. As I began to write "I Peed & Forgot" a few years ago, it made me think about everything I had been through along the way; the challenges, the opportunities, the lessons and the blessings. Through it all, I am still here. I started to wonder how could I help others learn from my bad experiences? Here was this terrible incident that people who didn't care about me know and use against me, so why not use it to help others? So, besides the book, in 2016, I decided to start my first company. I named it A Chip Off the Block after a saying Madear used about my brothers and me when people in the community would give her compliments on how well we behaved. She would always say in her sweet country voice, "They just a chip off the old block, Honey!" I feel blessed to have been raised by such a strong and beautiful soul who was so proud of us, even through our bad times. Madear loved helping others and truly was a great leader for my family. I want to use my company to help others learn some of what I learned from her, as well as from my own experiences--to know they are not alone and there are resources available to all of us if we just take the time to look. (Being able to share my story to help others be successful at what they do is what drives me to share this message with you.)

I also hope to bring greater awareness of the power of community service as a way to uplift neighborhoods. It helps all of us when we help our youth set high goals for themselves and dream big, no matter what their background or race is. I am proud to be putting my time and energy into this work, and making a living doing what I love. As a former professional athlete, in addition to this book and other materials designed to help others, I offer consulting, speaking, and leadership workshops to help educate and prepare leaders for the expected and unexpected in life and their careers. It took me years to know what that meant, and I like the idea of helping others learn it sooner.

I thank God for my experiences. I thank God for the blessing that football has been to my life, the doors it opened, and all the lessons I have learned along the way. It wasn't easy, but all of those things have molded me into the man I am. I accept full responsibility for the good and the bad I have done in my life. I can't thank God enough for the opportunity He has given me, and or the fact that I'm still here, able to help, teach, and encourage, to be a motivation for people who aspire to be professional athletes, people who may struggle being a single parent, or struggle with addiction—anyone who wants to learn and grow to become the very best versions of themselves.

I supposed this book—all the crazy events that have brought me to this clarified passion for helping others—has led up to my discovering & developing the principles that I call the "3E's," which are words that I feel are important in uplifting others and in making a difference in your community. **Expose** under-served people to resources that are available to them and how to access them. **Encourage** all to believe in their dreams/goals through positive reinforcement, proper planning, and help executing planned strategy. **Elevate** others and their community positively through civic service and involvement. These three principles mean a lot to me, and could make a difference in someone's life, who in turn could impact the world.

I've learned I can be a resource for a lot of people in many different challenging situations and I want to be an edifier to others. I just pray and hope I continue to grow. Isn't that the way it's supposed to be? 2 Corinthians 1:3-4, *"All praise to God, the Father of our Lord Jesus Christ. God is our merciful Father and the source of all comfort. He comforts us in all our troubles so that we can comfort others. When they are troubled, we will be able to give them the same comfort God has given us."* (NLT) I'm not perfect and I know I won't always do things perfectly, but God has brought me through all and still loves. It's my duty to share the same encouragement that helped me make it through the good and bad in my life. I think trying to live this out is what is going to continue making me a better person. I'm going to be honest with those around me, but most importantly to myself.

EPILOGUE:

Closing Letter

To my three beautiful children—I love you more than anything in this entire world. I pray every day for your health, and that one day you will be able to fully understand how important you all are to me. I have no doubt you will be able to accomplish any goals you set for yourselves, and I will do whatever I can to expose, encourage, and elevate to help you reach those goals. I hope you will someday be able to understand that I am not perfect, but I am still able to set and attain high goals despite setbacks. Looking back, there are so many things I would have done differently—most of the things that I regret affect you all directly.

For many reasons, which you read about in this book, I can't feel too much regret about the lessons I've learned, and I hope you'll look at your own lives this way, too. Challenges make you stronger!

Despite the many setbacks in life you will encounter, there comes the opportunity to learn, grow, and maybe help someone else who is going through something similar. Know that the people you are the closest to can potentially hurt you the most, but they will also love you the most unconditionally. The ones who love you unconditionally will always be there, no matter the situation. I also want you to learn from my experiences so you can avoid those who are your "friends" for the wrong reasons. You may find that some people are with you as long as things are going well, but put you down as soon as you hit life's rough patches. You will not always be able to identify those people at first, but knowing ahead of time that it's a possibility can definitely help you be more prepared when you find yourself faced with that kind of adversity. I feel that you all are old enough to understand this. In this book, I have opened up parts of my life and things about our family that you need to know to be successful. Not all will be positive about this book, but I know my intentions and my heart, therefore I have no regrets opening up to you and people who read this.

On your path to success, I encourage you to set high goals for yourselves. Make them almost unattainable! People around you will try to put doubt into your minds and minimize your dreams because they're not capable of believing. I heard a great Proverb that says, *"In their hearts human beings plan their lives. But the Lord decides where their steps will take them."* (Proverbs 16:9, NIRV) It's good and right to plan, but be willing and humble enough to adjust if the Lord wants to take you to somewhere unexpected.

Turning a dream into a reality takes courage, faith, hard work, and a lot of discipline, trust me. You can lose your dream way too soon if you don't prepare yourself as best as you can for a life that few dare to reach for. I learned the hard way that when you make a lot of money, personal issues in your life get ignored. Money does not solve all of your problems and please don't date or feel the need to be close to a person just because of how much money they have. Not only will you realize that money can't buy happiness, but you will also notice how many rich people are self-absorbed. I was the most miserable I have ever been while I was in the NFL. Everyone assumed that I was rich just because I was in the NFL. It's actually the opposite. Most professional football players are not rich and without proper mentoring/leadership they will leave with more debt than they came with.

Please keep spirituality close to your heart, because it helps you maintain inner peace and happiness. You know that my faith lies in Jesus. I want you to be you and find your faith too. As you search and grow in your faith, don't be judgmental. Being a real person means being tolerant and respectful of people of different backgrounds. I know it's hard considering how society is today, but I promise there is a greater good living a selfless life. Religion has so many people in this world fighting and judging one another over what higher power is the true one, but that's not the point. Pray God will show you the Truth, that's what I pray for you. I trust He will.

It's totally up to you as an individual to become as great or as spiritual as you want to be. Keep an open mind about learning and don't be afraid to fail. As I learned, failure keeps you humble and teaches you about yourself. My failures have taught me just as much about my true self, maybe even more, than my greatest accomplishments in life. Most people will encourage you not to try new things, because they want to keep you on the same basic, regular mind set they're on. It's in your DNA to dream big, be different, and follow your own path.

The last piece of advice I'd like to give is to remember not to take yourself too seriously. Make sure you are able to laugh at yourself, even in difficult times. Laughter has gotten me through some of my darkest days, and it also has kept me grounded, too. It is good for the heart, mind, and soul. I promise it makes your life better when you're able to smile through some of the most difficult times.

Rayn, at the point you saw me at my worst, thanks to alcohol and poor decision-making, i truly felt that there was nothing positive that could come from it. Strangely, the peeing event triggered something inside that I had not felt for a long time. I had forgotten who I was. It allowed me to face my fears, tell my truth, and begin traveling down a path that has finally brought me to a better place and a better relationship with you. I hate that something that negative had to happen and that you have had to deal with the horror of seeing your dad in that position. But I also have to be grateful that it happened when it did because it became a turning point in my life. Years of negativity had twisted my brain to focus on the bad more than the good, and I lost myself along the way. Sometimes taking a step back is the best thing that can happen to us if we listen carefully. Don't forget who you are! There will be times that you do, but get to know yourself as best you can and you'll find your way back in time. It is very difficult preparing for something that you have never experienced, so please take my story seriously.

I'm excited to see how your lives will play out for you, and I pray that God will protect you all while you navigate through your journey.

Love, Dad

CPSIA information can be obtained
at www.ICGtesting.com
Printed in the USA
BVOW03s0123300817
493487BV00001B/23/P

9 781524 551780